CVs and Applications

How to present yourself on paper

Patricia McBride

Student Helpbook Series

HOBSONS

CRAC

Acknowledgments

I would like to thank the following people for so generously giving their time, advice and assistance in preparing for this book: Samantha Sherratt, Yasmin Sherratt, Philip McBride, Simon Kime, Cambridge Careers Office, Margaret Wood, Robin Spence, Georgina Elton, Peter Bux, Lisa and Alix Findlay.

Thanks also to Royal Mail and UCAS for kindly allowing me to reproduce their forms.

© Hobsons Publishing PLC 1994

ISBN 1 85324 826 6

A CIP catalogue record for this book is available from the British Library.

CRAC

The Careers Research and Advisory Centre (CRAC) is a registered educational charity. Hobsons Publishing PLC produces CRAC publications under exclusive licence and royalty agreements.

Printed in England by Clays Ltd, St Ives plc

Cover artwork by Peter Froste
Text illustrations by Tim Oliver
Text design by Leah Klein

Ref. L156/B10qq/B/JE

N. 140904

Contents

How to Use this Helpbook

This Helpbook is for anyone who is applying for a job or college place. It will show you how to present yourself on paper so that you stand the best possible chance of getting an interview. The work you do to complete the application form and write your covering letter will be invaluable at the interview stage too, where it will act as a revision aid. This Helpbook will not, in itself, get you that job or place except on very rare occasions when colleges accept people without interview.

Each chapter is laid out in a similar way. At the beginning of the chapter there is a box that tells you what's in the chapter and when this information will be helpful. At the end of each chapter is a checklist to help you to review what you have just read and to act as a quick revision/reference guide.

Working through this book will help you to understand the whole process from beginning to end by:

- ◆◆ encouraging you to identify your strengths
- ◆◆ enabling you to present 'weaknesses' in the most positive way
- ◆◆ giving you the skill to handle difficult questions
- ◆◆ suggesting how to present yourself on paper in an appealing and eye-catching way.

The book takes you through these areas step by step and encourages you to be methodical in your approach. Some chapters contain exercises to help you to think through your application process. Doing them will save you a lot of time and effort later.

The book also contains:

- ◆◆ a reproduction of an UCAS form along with tips on how to complete one, or an application form for a college of further education

➡ a range of model CVs showing the various CV layouts you can use for different occasions

➡ two contrasting job application forms – one from a very big organisation and one from a small company with only eight staff

➡ several sample covering letters.

Because there are many common features in preparing for different types of applications, the background information to all of them is contained in Chapters 1 to 5.

Particular points needed for:

➡ CV layouts

➡ Job application forms

➡ College applications

can be found in the chapters of those names. In places in this Helpbook, icons (📖 and 💼) are used to indicate information of particular interest to those applying for a college place or a job.

Good luck with your application – if you follow the guidelines in this book your chances of success will be much improved.

1 Self-analysis

You should read this chapter:

- ↦ before you begin to complete an application form or write a CV.

By the end of this chapter you should know:

- ↦ how to analyse your skills and experience
- ↦ where to turn to for help with this analysis
- ↦ how to sell your leisure activities
- ↦ how to use words in a winning way.

Your goal

No employer would take on a new member of staff without interviewing them first. And whilst there are some colleges that don't interview prospective students and select them purely on the basis of their grades and application forms, they are still the exception. When you present yourself on paper in the form of a CV or an application form what you are trying to do is to sell yourself. This means that generally speaking *your goal in presenting yourself on paper is to get an interview*. All the information in this chapter is equally valuable for college or job applications as well as for compiling a CV.

So, let's have a good look at this product you have to sell – you! Imagine for a moment a person who has to interview candidates for a job or college place. He or she is looking to 'buy' (or select for interview) the best possible person. None of the people whose details have been sent in are known to him or her. Each person, at this stage, is simply a collection of facts. Initially the interviewer will be looking for some basic requirements:

- ↦ what you can offer

- your strong points
- your weak points
- your attributes in relation to other applicants.

These are the types of questions we will be looking at in relation to you during this chapter and Chapters 2 and 4.

Next the interviewer will look for:

- how well what you have to offer meets what he or she is looking for
- how effectively you have expressed what you can offer
- how you may be able to meet requirements if there is a skill or knowledge gap between what you can offer and what is needed.

These issues are covered further in Chapters 3 and 4.

'My skills'

Let's start your self-analysis on a positive note – your good qualities. This is probably, in fact, the most difficult

Sam finally admitted to a number of skills.

place for you to start because most people are far more ready to own up to their failings. However, it's got to be done, and rather like taking medicine, you feel good afterwards even if you cringe at the time. Once you've read the following lists of skills words or statements, it's a good idea for you to make notes of those which apply to you. You will find further suggestions to write in your own notebook as you work through this book.

Exercise

In your notebook, write a list of *everything* you can do. Things you can do are your *skills*. Here are categories of skills as a prompt – you will probably be able to add to them. To help you to remember all your skills (you may not have used all of them recently or consciously thought of them as skills), make a list of as many different tasks you have completed as possible. For example, did you undertake any projects at college or school which required skills not usually used? What skills have you used for studying or jobs you have done? What skills have you developed just from being with people or from helping around the house or with children?

Communication skills

- listening well
- speaking clearly
- speaking in groups
- writing legibly
- translating
- writing analytically
- beautiful handwriting
- writing concisely
- proof-reading accurately
- communicating clearly
- teaching others
- calming others
- explaining complicated ideas
- defending yourself verbally
- putting across an opposing viewpoint

Practical skills

- fixing cars
- typing
- carpentry
- cooking
- laying bricks
- sewing
- using a computer
- metalwork
- knitting
- filing
- driving
- applying first aid
- riding a bike
- plastering
- swimming
- painting
- demonstrating
- word processing

Financial skills

- budgeting
- calculating
- understanding the banking system
- paying bills
- evaluating
- analysing

People skills

- caring for disadvantaged people
- speaking in groups
- being empathetic
- advising
- supporting others
- liaising
- co-operating
- challenging
- leading
- organising
- team-building
- motivating
- caring for children

Creative skills

- drawing
- designing
- painting
- decorating
- inventing
- photographing
- modelling
- developing
- producing
- singing
- dancing
- composing
- choreographing
- acting
- playing an instrument
- writing creatively

Thinking skills

- editing
- analysing
- planning
- programming
- sorting
- devising
- designing
- preparing
- scheming
- shaping
- formulating
- originating
- conceiving
- imagining
- investigating
- researching
- enquiring
- questioning
- examining
- exploring
- inspecting

'My personality'

Once you have listed your *skills*, you need to consider positive aspects of your *personality*. Head up another sheet of paper in your notebook or a new file on your word processor and list all the words that describe your personality. It is hard for some people to apply positive adjectives to their personality so you might like to try the following exercise.

Exercise

Imagine that you are your best friend (or indeed a doting relative). He or she meets someone who explains that they have a vacancy for a job (or know of a college course) that sounds just right for you. They decide to strike while the iron's hot and do a selling job on your behalf. What would they say to the other person? How would they describe you? What skills would they highlight? What positive personal qualities would they mention?

Again, here is a prompt list. Note those qualities that apply to you and then add to them as necessary.

- kind
- sympathetic
- helpful
- consistent
- happy
- determined
- strong-minded
- willing to learn
- caring
- patient
- adaptable
- persistent
- resolute
- courageous
- adventurous
- sharp-witted
- resourceful
- lively
- academic
- observant
- mature
- careful
- glamorous
- sophisticated
- methodical
- elegant
- energetic
- bold
- dynamic
- imaginative
- charitable
- thoughtful
- empathetic
- diligent
- reliable
- humorous
- assertive
- flexible
- open-minded
- supportive
- honest
- responsible
- obliging
- cheerful
- considerate
- intelligent
- capable
- active
- quick-witted
- charismatic
- charming
- tenacious
- circumspect
- smart
- tidy
- fair
- stable
- modest
- co-operative
- straightforward
- creative
- perceptive

'My experience to date'

Your list of experience should overlap to some extent with your list of skills. If you are thinking 'what experience?', remember all the different things you have done.

What jobs have you had? Even a Saturday job counts, of course. Have you:

- ➥ done any voluntary work?
- ➥ undertaken work shadowing?
- ➥ had special responsibility at school or college?
- ➥ had special responsibilities at home?
- ➥ travelled?
- ➥ had responsibilities as a member of a club?
- ➥ done something unusual?

All of these experiences will have provided you with something relevant to offer an employer or college, if only something to talk about at interview (but more on that later).

Let's look at three quite different examples. For the first, let's assume that you worked for two weeks as a receptionist in a hotel as part of work shadowing. Most receptionist jobs involve:

1. attending to residents
2. checking residents in and out
3. answering the phone.

Sometimes receptionists also undertake other office work – typing, etc. If we break down these examples we see that each has required more skills than was immediately obvious:

Attending to residents requires you to:

1. have good communication skills
2. work with members of the public
3. be courteous
4. be patient
5. be able to respond to queries, sometimes at short notice
6. be able to cope with crises (double booking, people getting ill, etc)
7. keep calm.

Checking residents in and out requires you to:

1. be methodical
2. write legibly
3. communicate clearly
4. respond to queries
5. liaise with others
6. be pleasant
7. be organised.

Answering the phone requires you to:

1. have a good telephone manner
2. take accurate messages
3. respond effectively to the caller
4. deal with queries
5. be efficient
6. speak clearly and concisely.

By looking at your experience in this way, you may also discover some skills you hadn't thought of before. Remember, a skill is simply something you can do. For example, it is a real skill to handle crises situations effectively and not everyone can be pleasant with awkward customers for eight hours at a stretch.

A second example might be newspaper delivery. On one level it seems a fairly humble occupation; after all, quite young adults take on this job. However, let's analyse the skills and personal qualities involved:

Newspaper delivery involves:

1. being prompt and reliable
2. being able to work unsupervised
3. being efficient – delivering the right paper to the right house
4. being responsible for collecting money
5. being honest
6. keeping accurate records of money collected
7. being polite to customers.

Thirdly, imagine you are a 'returner' to the work-place. You may have been at home looking after the house and the family prior to and during your studies. If so, you have many skills to offer:

House-spouse and parent demands:

1. reliability (collecting the kids on time, etc)
2. budgeting (unless you're very lucky!)
3. creativity (play and so on)
4. patience (a vital skill for any parent and worker)
5. chairing skills (play group association, for example)
6. meeting skills (parent-teacher association, for example)
7. interpersonal skills
8. understanding child development
9. ability to multi-task (do several things at once)
10. letter-writing skills (to schools, etc)
11. attention to detail
12. keeping calm under pressure.

Getting help with your analysis

Undertaking an analysis of your positive points can be a difficult task. For this reason you may like to think about getting help from others. Obviously, you need to ask people you can trust and who will give you an honest answer. Also, it makes sense to ask more than one person. Choose people who see you in different circumstances – a friend you socialise with would not see you in the same way as a teacher or employer for example. Don't take everything people say at face value – really think about their comments. Do you agree with them? What examples could you give to back up the qualities or skills they have highlighted?

Using your Record of Achievement

Many students now have a Record of Achievement (RoA) which documents their academic and personal progress throughout their school career. If you have a RoA, you should find much material in it that can be utilised when writing CVs or completing application forms. You may be able to use it to reflect on your skills and personal development throughout the years – particularly in areas relevant to the job or course you are applying for.

Recording your education

Whether you are applying for a college place or a job, you will need to identify and record your education in a coherent and easy to read manner. If you are applying for a place at university you have little choice about how to display your educational achievements. The section of the UCAS form relating to examination results is shown on the page opposite.

However, Chapter 6 contains hints to ensure that you complete the form as effectively as possible.

If you are recording your education on a job application form or CV, on the other hand, you have much more discretion. Here are some tips to consider:

- ⇥ it is not usual to show your examining board on job application forms or CVs
- ⇥ you generally start with the highest level qualifications you possess and work 'down' through the list
- ⇥ list first those subjects that relate to the job you are applying for
- ⇥ be consistent with the way you show this information (more on this in later chapters)
- ⇥ if you have qualifications that are unusual in some way (perhaps obtained overseas), you might like to consider letting the reader know their British equivalent. Whilst this information is available to universities, most employers would not know where to start looking for it!

6	ACADEMIC QUALIFICATIONS										

6A Examinations or assessments for which results are known (other than those awarded by BTEC/SCOTVEC/NCVQ)

Examination Centre number and name

Examination			Subject	Level	Result Grade or Band	Examination			Subject	Level	Result Grade or Band
Month	Year	Board				Month	Year	Board			

6B Examinations or assessments to be completed, or results pending (other than those awarded by BTEC/SCOTVEC/NCVQ)

Examination			Subject	Level	(i) GCE/SEB/GCSE Examination Centre number and Centre address or (ii) title of examination	Institution use	
Month	Year	Board				Req'd	Actual

6C Qualifications awarded by BTEC/SCOTVEC/NCVQ

Unit, module or component title	Month/ Year taken	Level	Value	Results (where known)

Title of Award held	Qual'n	Title						
Title of current qualification	Qual'n	Title		Completed				
BTEC registration number for current qualification								
Name and brief address of college								

Unit, module or component title	Month/ Year taken	Level	Value	Results (where known)	Unit, module or component title	Month/ Year taken	Level	Value	Results (where known)

●→ do not abbreviate this information unless absolutely essential or unless the terms are very well known (for example, everyone knows what a GCSE is, but not everyone would know that Dip SW means the Diploma in Social Work).

Selling your leisure interests

So, how does recording your leisure interests help you with the application process? To answer this, let's look at university and job applications separately for a minute, then we'll look at ways in which you can write this section to best effect.

University applications

The UCAS leaflet *Instructions on How to Complete the Application Form* suggests interests you could mention in 'Section 10: Further Information'. These include:

- the background to your interest in the subject(s) applied for
- particular interests that you have in your current studies
- your social, sporting or other interests and activities
- details of any non-examined subjects that you are studying.

This, then, is your opportunity to sell your leisure interests. Read on to learn how.

One applicant had written under "Leisure Interests", "My main hobby is completing application forms". It made me laugh at the time but then I started thinking that this person might be too flippant. Not only that, but the comment seemed to imply he'd been applying for dozens of jobs. Why hadn't he been getting them?

Quote from an employer

Job applications and CVs

Most application forms have a section headed 'Leisure Interests' or something similar, so obviously this is where you present this information. If, however, there is no such heading and you particularly want to tell the organisation about a leisure interest that is relevant to the job, you can always mention this in the covering letter you send with your form (Chapter 9 covers this in more detail).

Likewise, most people include a section in their CVs headed 'Leisure Interests' or sometimes 'Additional Information'.

 One applicant for a job as community care assistant said "I like to knit and sew and yes, I even enjoy ironing". I suppose she thought that she would be an old-fashioned home help but the job has changed a lot. To me this said that this person knew little about what the job involves these days. She should have read the job description more carefully before putting pen to paper.

Quote from a local authority employer

Presenting leisure interests

When you think about completing this section, ask yourself what the person reading it will be looking for. Some possible answers are:

➼ a sense that you are a 'rounded' person. This means that you have both solitary and social activities and a reasonably wide range of interests. This, it is hoped, indicates that you are able to work alone and/or with others.

➻ something to talk to you about in the interview. (This is especially important for university and college interviews when many applicants are saying similar things on their forms. The fact that you did something unusual will give the lecturer something to talk to you about.)

➻ possibly, that your leisure interests in some way reflect the course or job you are applying for. This may be with a particular skill (for example, a practical hobby when applying for a practical job). Some employers actually say that this is the only thing they look for under this section. As you will not know in advance which approach to take you could consider putting any directly relevant interests first in your list. If you put the others first the reader might have stopped reading before they get to the good bits. Alternatively, it may be that the employer is looking for a personality trait that would be useful in the job (playing football may show that you work well as part of a team).

How to present 'interest' information

For many people, finding something to say under this section is really difficult. You think to yourself, 'Well, all I do is watch television and go out with my mates!' Oh dear, this is when you remember all those times your teachers and parents said to you, 'You really should join something instead of sitting around every evening!'

Still, let's see what we can make of your leisure activities that will look interesting to the reader.

Let's look at a fairly common example first:

'Watching television and going out with my mates'. What does it say about you? Answer these simple questions:

➡ What type of television programmes do you like?
Sport? Natural history? Thrillers? Films? Game
shows? (might show an interest in general
knowledge)

➡ What do you do when you go out with your
mates? Drink? Go to the cinema? Attend sporting
events? Play sports? Go to concerts?

➡ Do any of your answers to the above relate in any way
to the job or course you are interested in? If so, how?

Once you've thought through these questions your
answer might now read:

'I enjoy watching television, especially sports programmes and detective stories. I also enjoy seeing films. I
socialise regularly with friends, often attending concerts
or going bowling.'

What does this tell the person reading it?

a) you follow some solitary pursuits (watching television)
b) you have several different interests (sports, detective
stories, music)
c) you enjoy being with other people

Darren and his friends enjoyed lively discussions about sport.

Here is another example:

'For the past six months I've been hitching around Europe with my friends.' This tells the prospective interviewer:

- ➤ you have initiative and courage
- ➤ you can find your way around (both literally and figuratively)
- ➤ you are independent
- ➤ you are flexible (unless you had the whole trip planned in rigid detail before leaving)
- ➤ you can budget (unless of course you frequently wrote home for more funds!).

Get the idea? Looked at this way, what may have seemed a good laugh and of no significance to your future career or education actually tells people quite a lot about you.

So, you could re-word this statement as:

'I enjoy travelling and recently spent six months working my way through Europe with three friends. I particularly enjoy meeting people from other cultures and the sense of challenge and change from day to day.'

Notice that these examples start with 'I'. The leisure interests section is an opportunity for you to sell yourself as a real person as opposed to a list of skills and qualifications. This is more effectively done by writing your interests as part of a personalised sentence rather than 'reading, swimming, socialising'.

Here are some other examples:

'I enjoy reading crime novels and watching science fiction films. I also like socialising with friends, often going to classical concerts or to cricket matches.'

'I am a keen sportswoman and belong to the school badminton team. I also play tennis and squash. I enjoy reading biographies and watching comedy films.'

'I enjoy model-making and belong to the local Model-Making Society. I like playing snooker and spending time with friends.'

'*I very much like writing and belong to our local writers' group. I also enjoy reading, particularly political novels and crime stories.*'

Exercise

Now that you've read this section, make a list in your notebook of *all* your leisure interests and spend some time working out the best way to present this information. Remember, your overall aim is to get an interview for that course or job.

By the way, don't worry if the leisure interest which springs into your mind is not something you do regularly. As long as you have done/do it often enough to be able to talk sensibly about it at the interview, you should be OK.

Winning ways with words

By now, you should have a fair idea of the type of information you should present on paper, although there are more tips in later chapters. But for now, let's look at how to show this material effectively.

You've already had some help here (look back to the beginning of this chapter where there were lists of words for different skills and qualities for ideas). Thinking of your qualities and skills, work through these lists until you are happy that you have expressed yourself as accurately and effectively as possible.

Now look at the way you've wrapped up those words. Is the overall picture positive and lively or a bit dead? Look at these two leisure interest examples:

'Reading, going to the cinema, socialising.'

Do you feel you know much about this person? Do they even enjoy these activities? Does her/his personality spring from the page? Compare that with:

'I enjoy reading, particularly thrillers and science fiction. I also like socialising with friends, going to the cinema and concerts.'

Still fairly brief, but much more of a flavour of the person. So, use some 'I' language from time to time, show that *you* are there behind the facts!

It can be quite difficult sometimes to think of positive words and you can end up repeating 'enjoy' several times! Here are some alternatives:

➤ enthusiastic about	➤ pleased with/about
➤ enthusiasm for	➤ keen on
➤ passion for	➤ eager to
➤ interest in	➤ excited about
➤ fascination for	➤ stimulated by
➤ attracted to	➤ delighted with/to/by
➤ curious about	➤ happy about
➤ like	➤ exhilarated by

Likewise, you can present your words positively by using the present tense. Simply the difference between:

'*Served customers and stocked shelves*' and
'*Serving customers and stocking shelves*'.

A small point, but somehow the present tense sounds more dynamic and appealing.

Exercise

Now that you have your list of interests and have considered how to make them sound really positive, write them into one or two sentences. Practise until you are confident they sell you well. Remember though that you may well have to re-write this section for each job as you decide to emphasise different aspects of your activities to suit the job.

Chapter Checklist

Can you answer the following questions about yourself yet?

Yes No Question

❏ ❏ **What skills do you have?**

❏ ❏ **What good things have you achieved?**

❏ ❏ **What makes you stand out from the crowd?**

❏ ❏ **How would your referees describe you?**

❏ ❏ **How would you describe yourself?**

❏ ❏ **What would you say are your strengths?**

❏ ❏ **What would you say are your weaknesses?**

❏ ❏ **What interests you?**

2 Evidence of Success

You should read this chapter:

- when you begin to think about what to write on your application form or CV.

By the end of this chapter you should know:

- how to 'sell' your achievements effectively
- how to present information about awards you have received
- how and where to show any 'extra special' information about yourself.

Selling achievements

Having identified your skills by working through Chapter 1, you can now begin to define them in a way that should impress any prospective interviewer. Do keep in mind that ultimately everyone is in business to supply a service, whether that is a banking service or a teaching service or anything else. Also, everyone is in the business of survival. A company will not survive if it does not make profits. A college will not survive if it takes mediocre students and develops a poor reputation. Therefore it stands to reason that everyone is looking for a candidate who is not only going to be successful themselves, but will be successful for the organisation taking them on. Professionalism is the name of the game whether you're applying for a Saturday job or a postgraduate place at university.

All this means that prospective interviewers will be on the look out for people who have that something extra. And very effective 'extras' are those special attributes that bring some degree of fame and glory and which are measurable.

> I can't believe how many sloppy application forms I receive with no evidence of success in any form at all. Surely applicants must realise that it's a competitive world out there and we can afford to be really choosy who we interview.

Quote from a personnel manager

If you are at the very early stages of your career employers will not expect these 'extras' to be world shattering. Some examples of modest but still significant selling points can be found later in this chapter.

How do you show these extras? Well, you need to ask yourself in relation to each skill:

'*What evidence can I provide that is proof of my success in this area?*'

You do this by thinking in terms of *measurable* skills and abilities. Here are some examples:

- *how many*
  - ~ words you can type a minute
  - ~ software packages you can use
  - ~ people you served in a day
  - ~ items you can sort in an hour
  - ~ fraudulent credit cards you seized

- *how much*
  - ~ money you saved the organisation
  - ~ you earned for your organisation
  - ~ you sold last year
  - ~ time you saved by your new system

- *what percentage*
  - ~ of turnover you earned
  - ~ of total sales you made
  - ~ of time you saved by introducing a new process

- *how quickly*
  - ~ you delivered the newspapers
  - ~ you served the customers
  - ~ you learnt the new systems
  - ~ you learnt how to word process

- *how few/little*
  - ~ complaints you received
  - ~ costs you incurred
  - ~ waste you caused

Here are a few examples:

'*I acted in three school plays in the past two years.*'

'*My fund-raising efforts for the new school building reached £2,000.*'

'*I reorganised the layout of the magazines in the paper shop and this increased sales by 5%.*'

'*I reorganised the way the goods were processed through the stores department and this saved the company £3,000 per year.*'

'*The experiment I undertook in chemistry highers was later written up for the school magazine.*'

'*In two years I didn't miss a single day working at my Saturday job.*'

'*I was the supermarket champion for spotting people trying to pass stolen credit cards.*'

If you are applying for a university place then this sort of information becomes part of your 'Further Information'. The same would be true for an application form. For a CV, you can add this as the 'something special' in relation to a particular job or course. How to present this is covered in more detail in Chapter 6.

Kate found playing the lead in three school plays quite a challenge.

===== **Exercise** =====

Make a note of at least five extras you can include in your application form or CV. Try to present the material in a *measurable* format.

Special responsibilities

Have you held any special responsibilities at school, college, work or in your social life? These might include:

- being a prefect
- chairing meetings
- working on a committee
- being on working parties
- teaching others
- helping at events
- being a monitor
- looking after others
- producing a play
- organising a special event
- escorting guests around the school/college.

Again, many of these items suggest that you have that something extra, over and above the run of the mill person. Additionally, many of them suggest skills which may well be *transferable* to the job or course you seek.

Commendations, prizes and awards

The situation is very similar with commendations, prizes or awards. These might include:

→→ Queen's guide or scout
→→ Duke of Edinburgh Award
→→ Head Girl or Boy
→→ receiving an award for best dissertation
→→ music exams.

> One applicant had written under "Additional Information", "I speak Pidgin English". I couldn't understand what use that was to the job. If there was any relevance she should have expanded the point.

Quote from an employer

Do mention them even if they are not directly relevant. If there is nowhere else obvious for this information to go on your CV, you would write it under 'Additional Information'. If you have received any recognition it says something about you as a person. It suggests that you are:

→→ more motivated than most people, or
→→ more intelligent than most people, or
→→ more hardworking than most people, or
→→ more academic than most people, or
→→ more conscientious than most people

and that can't be a bad thing.

Articles written

If you have ever had anything printed that you have written, mention it. People are always impressed.

Where you write this information will depend rather on how relevant it is to the course or job you are applying for. Looking at university applications first, if the published material is very pertinent to the course, weave a mention of it into the body of your text. If not, you might add it as a final brief sentence at the end of your text.

The same rule generally applies to application forms. If there is nowhere to write it but it's important to mention, do so in the covering letter.

For CVs the situation is different. Make a new heading, 'Articles Published', and list each there. You should give the following information across one line of text for each article:

1. Name of article/book
2. Where published
3. When published

'Training Methods'   *Training Monthly*   June 1994

Add a very brief explanation of the content of the article if it is not clear from the title, eg:

'Training Methods' – an overview of the variety of methods available to the trainer when designing a course.

Exercise

Make a note of any:

- ◆▸ special achievements
- ◆▸ special responsibilities
- ◆▸ awards
- ◆▸ publications

you want to mention on an application form or CV.

Chapter Checklist

❏   Can you identify those successes you have had in your school or academic career in which an employer or college would be interested?

❏   Can you identify those successes you have had in your working life that would be interesting to an employer?

❏   Are you exceptionally good at one particular skill?

❏   Do you have more knowledge than other people about a particular area?

❏   Have you noted any special responsibilities you have undertaken?

❏   Have you received any awards or commendations?

❏   Have you ever had anything published?

❏   When you have identified your evidence of success, can you work out the most effective way to present it on your application form, CV or covering letter?

3 Selling Yourself on Paper

You should read this chapter:

↔ before you begin to complete a job or college application form or write a CV.

By the end of the chapter you should know:

↔ how to research the person who will read your information
↔ how to catch the busy reader's eye
↔ practical considerations for perfect paper presentation.

Getting your application read

By now you should have realised that you need to get inside the mind of the person reading your application form or CV if you are to grab their attention. Let's look at this in more detail.

Most colleges receive many more applications than they have places, perhaps eight times as many. But this figure pales into insignificance when you consider how many people apply for each job, especially in times of high unemployment. It is not unusual for companies to receive one or two hundred applications. One London organisation, advertising for a personal assistant, received 250 phone calls between 9 am and 2.30 pm.

So imagine yourself in their shoes. They are busy people, probably feeling totally overwhelmed by the number of applicants they must deal with. What do you imagine they could do to sift through this enormous mass of paper? Believe it or not, here are some of the stories I have heard:

- ◆ Some people discard CVs that are not accompanied by a covering letter.
- ◆ Some people throw away all CVs received after the cut-off date.
- ◆ One boss gave his secretary all the CVs. Her instructions were that *without reading them* she should discard those she didn't like the look of for any reason.
- ◆ Some people look at only the first 25 or whatever.
- ◆ Some people look only at one aspect of the form or CV depending on what they consider important. If this section doesn't exactly fit what they have in mind they ignore the lot, however good everything else is.
- ◆ Some people discount applicants who look unusual in some way (foreign name, for example, although this is actually illegal).

Thoroughly depressed yet? With stories like this you can feel like giving up. But, think positive. Although you can do nothing about the prospective boss who objects to surnames beginning with D, you can make sure that your application form or CV is neat and easy to read, that it is accompanied by a covering letter and that it arrives before the deadline for submission. You can also vastly increase your chances of getting your application *read*. Here's how to go about it.

Researching the reader

Applying for college places
Imagine that you are a college lecturer wading through a huge pile of UCAS forms. What would you be looking for?

1. The right qualifications or expectations of same.
2. Something in the application form that shows a real interest in the course and/or college applied for.

3. Something in the application form that would give the interviewer something to talk to you about at interview.
4. Something that makes you stand out from the crowd – but not too much.
5. A favourable report from your head-teacher.

Here is what one college lecturer who interviews many prospective students for an architectural course has to say:

People need to write something to catch my eye. A bland list of exam successes gives little to talk about during the interview. I like to see something in their application form about their experience in architectural study, even if it's a comment that they had a holiday somewhere and enjoyed looking at the architecture.

'It can be quite helpful to know where their interest in the subject comes from. Are other family members in architecture in some way? Did something else trigger off the interest?

'Leisure interests can be quite important too. If they don't show any I would wonder if that meant that they were working so hard at school they had no time for relaxation. This may indicate that they would not be able to keep up with higher level study. Some colleges are very keen on people with sporting interests because the college may want to maintain its reputation for sport. The same would be true for other areas such as music, so it's worth students considering if they have any of these skills which the college would value but which are not part of the course they are applying for.

'I get very turned off if the school report is poor. Sometimes it seems as though the writer is really struggling to think of anything positive to write at all. I appreciate though that this may say as much about the teacher's ability to write as it does about the applicant. I would advise students to ask to see a copy of the report in draft form and to ask for alterations if at all possible. They should try to get someone who's interested in them to write the report because it will pay off.

'When completing the form, students should keep in the back of their mind at all times that they should offer clues as to topics to discuss at interviews. Mind you, these should be real interests or they could end up with egg on their face on the day!

James remembered to offer a clue to his interests.

What this interviewer shows is that you need to research not just the reader and the course but also the college and its traditions. Ask around at school and elsewhere. Does anyone have personal knowledge of the college or the lecturer? One of the teachers? A student from previous years? The parent of another student? What can you read up about the college? Have the lecturers in your particular subject had anything published that you can study?

Applying for jobs

The first piece of research you should do on the reader of

your application or CV is to find out who that will be. The choice is generally between the manager who will interview for the job (and probably line manage the successful applicant) and someone from the organisation's personnel department. Smaller companies often do not have a personnel department. However, if one exists they usually handle at least the practical paperwork side of recruitment. That means placing the advertisement, responding to requests for applications forms and receiving incoming forms and CVs.

In most companies, these tasks will be done with the close co-operation of the departmental head involved. This means they should work together on:

- checking that the job description is up to date
- ensuring the person specification is accurate
- wording the advertisement
- making decisions about short-listing.

(The best ways to make effective use of the job description and person specification are covered in more detail in Chapters 6 and 8, and also in Chapter 9 on covering letters.)

Whether your application form or CV is read by a personnel manager or departmental head, they should be looking for the same things. That is, factors in your application that match their requirements.

Unfortunately, in times of high unemployment there may be many people who meet these requirements and this is when your research of the reader can help you to stand out from the crowd. Your research should concentrate most on the manager who will be short-listing. This is usually the person for whom the successful candidate will work. You can probably get this information either from the advertisement, the organisation's switchboard or personnel department.

Can you find out anything about this person without being too obvious? Ask around.

- Do you know anyone who works for the organisation?
- Can your local careers office or Jobcentre advise you?
- Does the company have a newsletter which you can request from the switchboard operator?
- Is there any information about the person from any material sent with the application form?

It may be something quite small that will ring a bell with them when they read your application form. Do you have any shared hobbies? Did you go to the same college or school? Do you belong to the same clubs or societies? Whilst it might be unwise to push this too hard on your application or CV you should certainly ensure that you mention it.

Imagining the reader

If you can't find out anything about the reader, try to imagine the sort of person she or he is likely to be. Whilst this process can be fairly fraught with poor guesses, it may help you to decide whether or not to include a piece of information about yourself.

Catching the busy reader's eye

Up until now this chapter has concentrated on the content of what you write. Now is the time to consider the presentation of your pieces of paper. Remember, many busy readers will be put off if you offend their eye in some way. Here are some tips to bear in mind:

- Always follow the instructions on application forms *exactly*. Read them through at least twice before you do anything.
- Make several photocopies of application forms so that you can practise on spare ones. It's worth every penny.

- Make sure that you write legibly.
- If you type the form or CV make sure there are no typing errors.
- Keep the form or CV spotlessly clean.
- Be consistent in the way you present material.
- Make your application form or CV look inviting to read.

One form arrived with a big coffee stain on it. The applicant had written on the form next to it, "Sorry, my daughter got at the form when I wasn't looking". I wasn't impressed. She should have kept the form safe, and if that failed phoned for another one.

Quote from a manager short-listing for a senior secretary's post

It can be difficult to complete an application form on a word processor because of the difficulties of aligning your text with the numerous lines and boxes. However, if you are preparing a CV try hard to get it word processed.

The advantages of a word processor are:

- you can easily make alterations or move text around
- they spell check for you!
- some can even check your grammar
- they have a thesaurus to help you select just the right word to convey your meaning
- you don't have to re-type each time so you can easily adapt the material in your CV for different jobs
- you can vary the type size and font (type of print).

But, don't:

- ➤ use too many fonts on the same document or it will begin to look messy (three is generally considered the maximum)
- ➤ go crazy with font sizes; be consistent with what size you use for what information
- ➤ use a font that is difficult to read, for example:
  - ~ a script font as they are hard to read and rather informal for a business letter
  - ~ a sans-serif font ie a typeface without adornments on the main strokes, unless you are applying to an informal or creative company. Not all employers approve of 'modern' typefaces.

Modern – it is, and I quite like it, but it's not that easy to read.
BrushScript – a pretty font, but you're not writing a love letter, are you?
LetterGothic – don't like this much; looks like an old typewriter.

- ➤ use too many different ways of emphasising information. Your choice is:
  - ~ underlining, or
  - ~ making text bold, or
  - ~ making text italicised, or
  - ~ altering text size.
- ➤ be inconsistent with how you use the above ways of emphasising points.

Here are some fonts you may like to consider:

---

1. Palatino – easy to read, but perhaps a little informal.
2. NewsGothic – a pleasant, straightforward font.

3. NewCentury Schoolbook – this is a commonly used font.

4. Times – compact and easy to read as the name would suggest.

5. **Helvetica – easy to read, though not recommended for all applications.**

6. **Bookman – pleasant, easy on the eye.**

7. Book Antiqua – a nice typeface, although slightly out of the ordinary.

8. Garamond – another popular, attractive face.

CV page layout

If you don't know anyone with a word processor, agencies will produce your CV for a reasonable cost if you have prepared it in a thorough and uncomplicated way. Here are some points that will help whether you type/word process it yourself or use an agency:

There is much more information about CV layouts in Chapter 8, but here are some general points:

- don't make your CV look cramped; leave plenty of 'white space'
- leave a good margin around your text, about an inch
- generally use single spacing, but double between paragraphs
- if using a typewriter, make sure that the ribbon doesn't need replacing
- be consistent in the way you present information – make reading as easy as possible
- use good quality paper – 80gm at least
- always keep in mind – 'Does this look like a document I would want to read?'

By the way, keep some spare paper. You should write your covering letter on the same stuff!

Chapter Checklist

When presenting yourself on paper, have you:

❏ Identified the reader?

❏ Tried to get inside the mind of the reader?

❏ Remembered that the reader is busy and may be easily put off?

❏ Found out as much background as you can about the place you're applying to?

❏ Made sure that all your information is provided in a logical, methodical and easy to read manner?

❏ Tried to get your application form typed or your CV word processed, if possible?

❏ Left lots of 'white space'? Remember not to squash too much information on to the page.

❏ Ensured that your application form, CV or letter is spotless, with no coffee stains, crossings out, etc?

❏ Used good quality paper?

❏ Used the same paper for your covering letter as for your CV?

4 Overcoming Common Problems

You should read this chapter:

◆◆ prior to completing application forms or CVs if you feel you have any 'difficult' information to provide.

By the end of this chapter you should know:

◆◆ how to present a variety of potentially difficult information in a way that is positive, or at least limits the damage.

Golden rules

It is unfortunately fairly rare for anyone to be able to look at an advertisement for a job (or a job description) and be able to say, 'This was written for me!' In this chapter we will look at how to get around the lack of ideal fit between what the employer wants and what you've got. But first of all, two golden rules.

The first one is, if you really like the look of a job, *go for it* even if it appears that you are less than ideal. What have you got to lose? Even if you spend time completing an application form or CV just to be rejected, you can use the work you put in for the next job. One thing you soon learn is that completing application forms can quickly become a chore. So working on one is never wasted because you can copy or adapt what you've written for the next form you complete.

The second rule is *minimise your problem.* Give the information you must provide but don't emphasise the gaps.

For example, what's the point in actually saying (perhaps in your covering letter) 'I know I don't have

the . . . you require, but I am very interested in this job.'
Let the reader find out by looking at your form. Never
point out the undesirable.

Too young

It's sadly true that we live in an ageist society. You will
undoubtedly find that some advertisements state that
they are looking for people older than you. Well, think
positive. Being too young is something that time will
cure easily.

If you are too young for an advertised job (or occasionally a course) apply anyway – remember golden rule
number one. In Chapter 8 you will find a way to write a
CV that excludes showing dates such as dates of birth.
However, your education and career experience dates
will be a quick give-away to anyone with even basic
mathematical skills and the likelihood is that you *will*
have to show this information, especially if you have to
complete an application form.

So, give the factual (date) information you have to,
but don't in any other way draw attention to your age
(such as by saying in your covering letter 'I appreciate
that I am two years younger than your stated preferred
age'). Remember, if an employer receives dozens, possibly hundreds, of applications, you will be making it easy
for them to reject your application unread.

Instead, just as you would do anyway, emphasise
what you *do* have to offer rather than your lack of years.
Make the most of your previous experience, thinking
through the issues around direct and transferable skills
really carefully. Do your best, then sit back and hope for
the reward of an interview. If all else fails, just wait until
the next time a similar job is advertised – your age may
have caught up by then.

Too inexperienced

You may have heard of the expression 'Catch-22'.

Basically, it means being in a no-win situation. Being too inexperienced is often a Catch-22 situation. You can't get the experience without the job and you can't get the job without the experience: stalemate. However, all is not lost.

In Chapter 1 you were asked to list *all* your skills and personal qualities. This is a time to consider which skills you have that may be transferable. That is, they may not be exactly the same as those requested, but they may show that you have similar abilities and aptitude. Let's look at some examples:

Example 1

As part of your last year at school you undertook some community service. You visited an elderly lady round the corner. You did a bit of shopping for her, read to her and generally kept her company. Now you're thinking that you'd like to apply for a job in a day nursery. In many ways the two seem quite different, but a lot of skills are general and transferable. Both require:

- getting on with people
- patience
- the ability to listen
- caring skills
- understanding another person's point of view
- trustworthiness
- communication skills.

Not a bad list and one that would interest any prospective nursery employer.

These are your *transferable skills* and are essential to any job that involves working with people. And think about that. It is not only in the 'caring' professions that you need to work with people. These skills would be equally valuable to a bank clerk, a doctor, a vet, a solicitor, even a car mechanic. Looked at from the customer's point of view, who would not be happy to deal with anyone in any profession who had these qualities?

Example 2

During a summer vacation while at college, you and three friends went hitching and working around Europe. You did a variety of jobs to earn enough money to keep travelling. They included waiting at table, washing up, and grape picking. Now, at the end of your course, you want to apply for a job as a management trainee for a finance house. Apart from your qualifications you can offer:

- experience of foreign currencies
- money handling experience (OK, on a smaller scale I admit)
- using your initiative
- working as part of a team
- being resourceful
- experience in European travel
- knowledge of other cultures
- personal budgeting skills
- crisis-handling skills (well, there probably would have been at least one, after all).

Zoe found her crisis-management skills invaluable in her new job.

These transferable skills would be invaluable in any number of other jobs, for example, banking, travel agencies, translating, social work, nursing, and teaching.

Get the idea? The jobs you are interested in may not actually specify these qualities, but it is worth looking carefully at the details of the job and thinking through the types of situation someone doing it might face.

Suppose you went to work in Tesco's as a trainee manager. Crisis-handling skills would be very valuable if you found yourself confronted with a shoplifter, someone using a stolen credit card, a severe staff shortage or a customer having a heart attack. Just because a job doesn't specify crisis-handling skills, it doesn't mean they don't have crises or won't think this an asset.

Health problems

There are no strict guidelines for disclosing health problems. There are, however, some which are 'traditionally' mentioned on application forms. These are health problems like epilepsy, and physical disabilities that may affect the way a job is done. Some other complaints, such as diabetes or slight hearing or visual problems, are 'invisible' and you should use your judgment about whether to mention them. This judgment could be based on the type of work you are applying for and the extent of your disability.

Legally, employers with over a certain number of staff must make up at least 3% of their workforce with disabled people. If you think this might actually work to your advantage, go for it. Your Jobcentre or careers office will be able to advise you.

Wrong qualifications

One of the really tough things about our education system is that we have to make choices about which subjects to take at a time when most of us haven't a clue what we want to do with our lives. This can mean that the choices we made at 14 can affect our chances of achieving the goals we set ourselves at 16 or 18 or 20. Well, unfortunately, we can't turn back the clock, so we have to work with what we've got.

If you are thinking of applying for a college place in a different subject area, ask yourself '*How can I sell this 'odd' application to the college?*' The lecturer in Chapter 3 said he looked for a real interest in the subject. Let's therefore imagine that you took all science subjects at school but now want to do an arts course. Why? How can you really convince the reader that this is an abiding interest and not just a passing whim? Can your head teacher or whoever writes the letter to your college back up your application with examples?

For some subjects, it would be very unlikely that you could get a place without prior learning and science would be one of these. Can you apply to a college which has an introductory year of some sort in your chosen subject area?

By the way, this is another situation where simply getting older helps. Many colleges are much more relaxed about entry qualifications for older students, believing that they have the self-knowledge and motivation to study hard and see the course through.

If you are applying for a job which specifies different qualifications to your own, many of the same points apply. How can you convince the prospective interviewer that, despite the 'wrong' qualifications you have sufficient knowledge and skill to handle the job? Do you have valuable experience if not the qualifications? Do you have similar, transferable skills? In times of high unemployment there are likely to be many people with the 'right' qualifications applying for a job, but remember – 'Nothing ventured, nothing gained'. You definitely won't get the job if you don't apply for it. If unemployment is low, employers can't afford to be so choosy and you will stand a much better chance.

Murky past

Do you have any skeletons in your cupboard? Did you:

- get expelled from school for cheating in an exam?
- skip lots of classes?
- get in trouble with the law?
- job hop for the past two years?
- get sacked from your last job?
- have a reputation for laziness?

Well, if you can answer 'yes' to any of these types of question, the next question has to be, *'Does anyone have to know?'* The answer is *'It depends'*. It depends on the sort of college place or job you are applying for.

If you got expelled or truanted a lot, for example, it may be mentioned in any letter or reference from your school to a college or employer and there is little you can do about that. However, if you are genuinely a reformed character and have had time to prove it, you could ask the teacher either not to mention earlier problems or to say how your situation and behaviour have improved.

For some jobs trouble with the law won't count, but with others they're vitally important. If you helped your dad with a bullion raid, a bank might think twice about you. Agencies working with children would definitely not look at you if you had a history of abusing children.

You should never lie on an application form or CV. But remember, some questions simply aren't asked at the paper stage and it is up to the interviewer to ask those questions at the interview itself. If you *do* have to write about these issues and they are part of your 'youthful indiscretion' as it is called, you may want to point out that you've grown up a bit since then and are keen to be successful in your chosen course or career.

Again, see if you can persuade someone to give you a reference that will confirm this.

Lack of leisure interests

Chapter 1 provides you with ideas on how to overcome any lack of 'desirable' leisure interests.

However, you should be wary of writing anything that might trigger prejudice in the reader. If this is the case, the 'Leisure Interests' section is where it is most likely to show. If you're an active member of a political party, for example, the reader's politics might not match your own.

Overcoming prejudice

One of the strange things about human beings is that we want two different things that are difficult to achieve at the same time. We want:

- to be treated as an individual to give us a sense of identity, and yet
- we also want to be treated as part of a group to give us a sense of belonging.

Sadly, for many people, being part of a group (their *in group*) is only significant if there is an *out group* to be against. Take football supporters, for example, or those supporting either Oxford or Cambridge teams in the boat race. For many people, to be *for* one thing means you must be *against* another.

This means that, unfortunately, most people are walking bundles of prejudice. It's just that different people are prejudiced against different things. We could, for example, be prejudiced against people with blue eyes or those with a second toe longer than their big toe. Luckily, most people have only mild prejudices and do not act on them.

However, there are some fairly common prejudices and these are usually based around easily observable *differences*. People are often fearful of others they see as in some way different. These differences include:

- ➡ ethnic origin
- ➡ gender
- ➡ religion
- ➡ sexuality
- ➡ age
- ➡ disability
- ➡ politics
- ➡ class
- ➡ lifestyle.

In Great Britain there is only legislation against discrimination on the grounds of gender or race. This means that these are the only two areas where you will have legal backing if you can prove discrimination. And proving such discrimination is a problem in itself.

The difficulty is that unless you know the person opening your envelope you don't know if you are dealing with a prejudiced person or not. I prefer to be optimistic and trust that people are fair. However, this is not always the case. There has been quite a lot of publicity about Asian law students who have tried to get work with law firms. Even the top students who have exceptionally high grades fail to get interviews. One such person, an Asian woman, was second in her year at college – a brilliant student. She applied for literally dozens of jobs and failed even to get an interview for most of them. She was eventually employed by a London Borough in their legal department. She is now in charge of the Equal Opportunities Commission!

Likewise, in some circles there is still prejudice against women (and occasionally against men). For example, one area manager in an insurance company said to his personnel manager when looking through application forms, 'Don't give her an interview. She's 32. In ten years' time she'll be menopausal.' There's still a long way to go before everyone is treated equally.

All of which leaves you with the need to make a decision about how to handle prejudice. Do you have a foreign sounding name? Are you are female applying for work in a traditionally male job market, or vice versa? How can you handle this? Some available options are:

- to avoid mentioning your religion or political beliefs in the 'Additional Information' section
- to avoid including interests that indicate your sexuality or lifestyle if these might be considered 'alternative'
- to consider using only initials on your application form
- if you have an unusual first name but a more ordinary second name, to consider using that name on application forms.

Of course, you shouldn't have to do this, but these are some of the options available.

If you are absolutely sure that you are being discriminated against, you can take your case up with either:

The Commission for Racial Equality
Elliot House
10/12 Allington Street
London SW1E 5EH
Tel: 071-828 7022

or

Equal Opportunities Commission
Overseas House
Quay Street
Manchester M3 3HN
Tel: 061-833 9244

You will find staff at both places very easy to talk to and willing to give advice. They also have a range of booklets about the subject that are free and very easy to read.

Chapter Checklist

❑ If you are really too young for the job you want, go for it anyway and let the employer know what a lot you have to offer.

❑ If you don't have sufficient experience, sell what experience you have hard and don't forget transferable skills from other areas of your ability.

❑ If you have health problems consider whether to disclose them or not. Some are always disclosed, others are discretionary. Get advice from your careers office or Jobcentre.

❑ If you don't have the right qualifications and are keen on the job, apply anyway. They may not get anyone with the right qualifications and even if they do you may have other attributes which they may consider more important.

❑ If you have some skeletons in your cupboard, think about how to present them in the best light. See if you can find someone who will give you a reference stating that you are a reformed character (assuming you are!).

❑ Think carefully about your leisure interests and how to present them. If you genuinely don't have any, get off the sofa and find some . . .

❑ Be careful about disclosing information which could arouse the reader's prejudice – comments about politics or religion, for example.

5   Filling in Your UCAS Form

You should read this chapter:

- ➡ when you are thinking about completing your UCAS or college of further education application form.

By the end of this chapter you should know:

- ➡ how to complete the factual section of your form
- ➡ how to present yourself positively in the 'Further Information' section.

UCAS application forms

Applicants for places on courses in universities and colleges of higher education have to complete a UCAS application form irrespective of which college they are applying for. However, colleges of further education each have their own application form and it would be impossible here to go into the detail of each one. For this reason, we will concentrate on the UCAS form which will have many of the same questions as you are likely to find with further education college forms.

Let's look through the UCAS form in some detail. As you will have already noticed, some sections are very straightforward and factual whilst Section 10 is a dreadfully empty page.

1   Title/name/address

This is very basic and the only thing to say here is to ensure that the information is easy to read and presented in a tidy and legible way.

By the way, you are asked for previous names so that institutions can link up your application with any previous records they hold.

UCAS

PO Box 67, Cheltenham, Glos. GL50 3SF

Attach your application fee and completed acknowledgement card here with a paperclip

APPLICATION FORM FOR ENTRY IN

- YOU MUST READ THE INSTRUCTIONS BEFORE COMPLETING THE FORM
- USE BLACK INK OR TYPE

333
4880686

1994

1 TITLE/NAME/ADDRESS	Title

2 PERSONAL DETAILS

Surname/Family name

First name(s)

Previous surname/family name

Correspondence address

Postcode (UK only)

Telephone (including STD code)

Home address (if different)

Postcode (UK only)

Telephone (including STD code)

Your age on 30 September 1994

Years   Months   Gender

Date of Birth

Date of first entry to the UK   Disability special needs

Area of permanent residence

Country of Birth

Nationality

Residential category

Sponsor/fee code

A   AS   H   C   W   P

BTEC HSC ILC M WR OEQ

3 APPLICATIONS

(a) Institution code name	(b) Institution code	(c) Course code	(d) Campus code	(e) Course code name	(f) Further requested details	(g) Prev Applic'n (year)	(h) Home	(i) Defer entry

Previous applicants through UCCA or PCAS please enter the serial or application number of your most recent application

4 EDUCATION FROM AGE 11	From Month Year	To Month Year	PT, FT or SW	UCAS SCHOOL OR COLLEGE CODE

5 PLANNING STATISTICS

A Occupational Background

B Ethnic Origin

2 Personal details

Your age on 30 September 19 . .
This is pretty self-explanatory!

Gender
It shouldn't be too difficult to answer this question!
UCAS probably require this information for their statistics, and colleges may need to know your gender for
accommodation purposes.

Date of birth
This should be in the usual British style – that is, day,
month, year. This is worth noting if you come from a
country where it's presented as month, day, year.

Date of first entry to the UK
Obviously, this question only applies to overseas students.

Disability/specialist needs
Note 16 of the *Instructions on How to Complete the
Application Form* gives you a choice of ten possible num-
bers to enter into this box.

Don't be afraid to give this information, it will not be
used in any way to consider your academic ability to
complete a course but is used to judge how well attempts
at equal opportunities for disabled students are progressing.

Area of permanent residence
Again, the *Instructions* leaflet gives you the categories to
use.

Country of birth
Write the current name of the country in which you were
born (not the name at the time of your birth).

Nationality
A nice straightforward question. The answer should be
obvious but if in doubt use the one on your passport,
assuming you have one.

Residential category
A small box here for you to enter the category which most closely describes you.

 It's such a pleasure to see a well presented application form. All interviewers try hard to be objective, but most of us start in a more positive frame of mind when faced with a form that looks good.

Quote from an admissions tutor

Sponsor/fee code
A box for two numbers using the appropriate code to show who is expected to pay your fees.

And that's the simple bit . . . Having said which the next few sections are still factual.

3 Applications
This is where you absolutely must turn to the *UCAS Handbook* before going further. The Handbook contains lists of the institutions and courses under the UCAS scheme. You can choose up to five courses, one per line. If you choose fewer than five courses you cannot add further choices to the scheme later, so think carefully before you leave any boxes empty.

4 Education from age 11
Here you are asked simply for:

- ◆◆ the name and brief address of the three most recent schools, colleges, polytechnics and or universities you have attended
- ◆◆ the dates of attendance
- ◆◆ whether attendance was part-time (PT), full-time (FT) or sandwich (SW).

6 ACADEMIC QUALIFICATIONS

6A Examinations or assessments for which results are known (other than those awarded by BTEC/SCOTVEC/NCVQ)

Examination Centre number and name

Examination			Subject	Level	Result Grade or Band	Examination			Subject	Level	Result Grade or Band
Month	Year	Board				Month	Year	Board			

6B Examinations or assessments to be completed, or results pending (other than those awarded by BTEC/SCOTVEC/NCVQ)

Examination			Subject	Level	(i) GCE/SEB/GCSE Examination Centre number and Centre address or (ii) title of examination	Institution use	
Month	Year	Board				Req'd	Actual

6C Qualifications awarded by BTEC/SCOTVEC/NCVQ

Unit, module or component title	Month/ Year taken	Level	Value	Results (where known)

Title of Award held	Qual'n	Title	
Title of current qualification	Qual'n	Title	Completed

BTEC registration number for current qualification

Name and brief address of college

Unit, module or component title	Month/ Year taken	Level	Value	Results (where known)

5 Planning statistics

This section is for UCAS to use for monitoring and planning purposes.

A Occupational background

This relates to the occupation of the 'highest income parent, step-parent or guardian in the household in which you have been brought up. If that person is retired, state the most recent occupation. Alternatively, if you are aged 30 or over please enter the occupation of the person who contributes the highest income to your household.'

This is good – a real equal opportunities question. Even now, many forms used for a variety of purposes only ask for the occupation of the man in the house, or the 'head of the household' – always assumed to be the man even if the woman earns more.

B Ethnic origin

Yes, we've all got one. You'd be surprised how many white, British people think it's only everyone else who is 'ethnic'.

Again, there is a code which best describes your ethnic origin. This information is not passed on to any institutions within the UCAS scheme.

Well, that's the first page done. On to the next page which should be completed in block capitals:

6 Academic qualifications

6A Examinations or assessments for which results are known

6B Examinations or assessments to be completed, or results pending

6C Examinations awarded by BTEC/SCOTVEC/NCVQ

You must write here all examinations taken or to be taken whether or not you have passed.

7 Record of Achievement

The form simply asks you to indicate if you have one.

8 Special needs

There is space here for you to enter any special needs.

OK, so that's the factual information out of the way. You should take a photocopy of the whole form, of course, as you will need to 'revise' what you said prior to interview because that's a large part of what you'll be questioned on. Whatever you do, TAKE A PHOTOCOPY OF THIS SEC-TION. You'll have to reproduce some of this information many times in your life and whilst at the moment, having slogged over your work for so long, you think you'll never forget the exact details, believe me you will. Imagine yourself at 40 scratching your head and thinking 'Now when did I take my geography A-level?'

 Schools are very good these days about giving a lot of help to students to complete the form in the best possible way. Despite that, some still come through which are dreary to read and fill me with no enthusiasm to meet the person.

Quote from a college lecturer

Here is what a lecturer in a teacher training college had to say about some of the application forms she has seen:

The applications from prospective student teachers include an application form, a covering letter and a letter of application. I will have received separately a ref-erence from their head teacher which the prospective stu-dent will not have seen.

'When I read through the forms prior to interview I look for a real commitment to wanting to teach.

Candidates must show that they have done some work with youngsters. I don't want to think that they have just decided "Oh, it might be a good idea to work with children". I need to see a real commitment to the work.

'I like to be convinced, even on paper, that there is a sense of real warmth towards children. That can come across even on the application form because of the way they describe the work they have done with children in the past.

'Sadly, some prospective students come across as very naive and not very politically aware. That is, they don't seem to know what's going on in the teaching world, they don't seem to have read the *Times Educational Supplement*, nor to be aware of current issues in education. We would like to see this type of awareness on the application form because we want to know that students know that the job is a difficult one and that finding employment at the end of the course is not easy.

'When I read through the forms they are sometimes so poor that I suspect that the applicants don't show them to anyone else before they send them off. I suppose it could feel a bit embarrassing for some people to do so, but it would be of real help to get an objective view before they put the form in the post. After all, they must know that people are going to read them at the college. If they did get someone else to check them, they wouldn't make such basic mistakes. They really need to find someone they can trust to go through their application form with them and to question them on it.

'For example, during the interview I will often take a phrase out of people's letter of application and start my question by saying, "You say in your letter of application . . .". This means that if they haven't thought through a statement they've made they can be left looking foolish at interview. When completing an application form, students should always have the interview in mind as well.

7	ROA	Do you have an up-to-date (post 16) Record of Achievement?	YES ☐	NO ☐

| 8 | SPECIAL NEEDS Physical or other disability or medical condition including any which might necessitate special arrangements or facilities | |

9 DETAILS OF EMPLOYMENT TO DATE	Nature of work	From		To		PT or FT
		Month	Year	Month	Year	

10 FURTHER INFORMATION

11 DECLARATION: I confirm that, to the best of my knowledge, the information given in this form is correct and complete. I have read the instructions, *in particular paragraphs 77–79.* I understand what they say, and I agree to abide by the conditions set out there, which I accept as conditions of this application.

Applicant's Signature	Date	This form must be accompanied by the fee of £12.00

'Sometimes after I've actually interviewed the person I feel a need to go back to re-read their application form to see if what they wrote ties up with what they were saying.

'With regard to references, sometimes I am horrified at the way they are worded. One head of department had written "This student is not academically bright but will make an excellent primary school teacher".

'One big question I always keep in mind – "Would I want this person to teach my child for a year?"

9 Details of employment to date

Just give brief details here of your employer, the nature of your work, the dates you were working, and whether the job was part-time (PT) or full-time (FT).

10 Further information

Now for that dreadfully empty page. The *Instructions on How to Complete the Application Form* leaflet provides you with some excellent headings on what to put in this section and the interview with a college lecturer in Chapter 3 may have also given you some ideas.

Oliver spent some time working out his word limit.

(This and other information in this section reproduced by kind permission of UCAS.)

Before you start, think about your word limit. Photocopy the page and write on two or three lines. There are 27 lines. Multiply these by the number of words you can write (or type) per line and you have your maximum word number (the leaflet tells you not to go on to a second page).

Many people really dread completing this section. But think of this as a piece of work: an essay. What do you do with any essay?

You:

- read the question and attempt to fully understand what is expected of you
- read all the relevant material to formulate an answer
- select those aspects of the material needed for your essay, rejecting those that are inappropriate
- plan how to present your information, considering all aspects, angles and arguments
- write an essay plan
- do a draft
- refine it as many times as it takes to get it right
- make a good copy.

And that's exactly what you have to do with this section. Don't even expect to polish it off in one sitting. Start the work and then leave it for a few hours or a day, mulling it over in your mind as you go about the rest of your life. Once you have decided on what to say, polish and polish it until it gleams. It should take you several goes.

Don't forget that in Chapter 1 there is a list of words for expressing positive feelings. You might want to refer to it when you get to the revision stage.

Remember, your work in completing this form is for two purposes:

- to get you an interview
- to give you something to talk about at the interview.

Hopefully, one will follow on smoothly from the other. If you have been working through this book you will already have in your notebook or on your word processor details of:

- your skills
- your experience
- your education
- your character
- your interests
- your leisure activities
- your strengths
- any special awards, etc.

You have also considered how to overcome common problems you might face.

Keeping in mind what the teacher training college lecturer had to say at the beginning of this section, do consider current issues in the area of your choice. You can get information on this from:

- your school
- professional or trade journals (your central library will probably have them)
- talking to people already doing the job your course could lead to
- newspapers and the media generally
- speaking to existing students.

Exercise

This is where you put together all this work in a sparkling and riveting way. How about this example opposite (I've numbered each paragraph for reference later).

1. I am applying for the Business Studies HND course because I am interested in business and I want a good career.

2. I have become interested in business because my father works in a bank and I realise that I must get a good qualification to start my career in a junior management position.

3. I worked in a building society for three weeks for work experience. I know that this isn't quite the same as a bank but I learnt a lot of useful things.

4. I am currently taking seven GCSEs including business studies which I enjoy very much. I particularly like learning about the way the financial world works

5. My ambition is to be a bank manager or to work for a large finance company.

6. I enjoy playing netball, and going to the cinema. I also enjoy embroidery and am a keen photographer.

7. I have just passed my First Aid Certificate with the British Red Cross.

8. I have not yet secured an industrial placement, but have applied to three banks and am awaiting their response.

9. I do not wish to defer my application to next year.

Work through the above information paragraph by paragraph. What is good about the information provided and in what ways could it be improved keeping in mind the course applied for?

Do not read any further until you have completed this exercise.

General points

The first thing to note is that nearly every paragraph starts with 'I' (not uncommonly seen on such forms). Try to make your beginnings more varied.

Further, the whole thing is a bit disjointed with no 'flow' to the content. Although it provides quite a lot of relevant information, it is stilted and uninspiring. Many of the points should be expanded further.

Specific points

Here are some suggestions as to how each paragraph could be improved. You may have thought of others.

1. *I am applying for the Business Studies HND course because I am interested in business and I want a good career.*

This is clearly far too brief an answer. The student should have mentioned:

➥ why he or she wanted this particular course rather than one run by any other college. This would include mentioning specific aspects of the course that may differ from those offered elsewhere. It may be relevant to discuss the type of college, the method of teaching or the college location if these have a particular bearing on the application.

➥ information about being interested in business and career aspirations should preferably be all in one place. In this example they are dotted around rather disjointedly.

2. *I have become interested in business because my father works in a bank and I realise that I must get a good qualification to start my career in a junior management position.*

It can be helpful to show that there is a family tradition of working in a particular field because:

➥ it shows that you are likely to have a deeper than average knowledge of the work

➥ you are likely to get support from your family

➥ you are likely to have realistic expectations about career structures.

However, the two halves of the sentence don't really 'hang together'. There are better ways to word this paragraph, but at the very least there should be a full stop after the word 'bank'. Perhaps the first half could read, '*I feel that I have a good understanding of business from a banking perspective as my father works in a bank. This means that I am very familiar with the type of work involved.*' It may even be helpful here to give examples, and in a completely re-written version these examples could be linked to the work experience in a building society.

The second half of the sentence would probably be better elsewhere – perhaps as part of the 'reasons for applying for this course' section.

3. *I worked in a building society for three weeks for work shadowing. I know that this isn't quite the same as a bank but I learnt a lot of useful things.*

Ouch! What a lot of missed opportunities here. For a start, never put yourself or your skills down; '*I know it isn't quite the same.*' The reader knows that too, there's no need to emphasise it. Here are some pointers about this section:

→ It doesn't give any feeling of enthusiasm. The person is saying they want to work in this type of environment, but gives no indication of having enjoyed it.

→ There is much overlap between working in a building society and working in a bank, especially as building societies offer many banking facilities. This means that this person would have learned many *transferable skills* that could have been mentioned. These would include:
  ~ dealing with people
  ~ handling money
  ~ filing
  ~ understanding systems
  ~ answering the telephone
  ~ liaising with other branches
  ~ using a computer.

➡ This section could also have mentioned those aspects of the work that the applicant particularly enjoyed and those he or she is keen to learn more about (ensuring of course that the course being applied for covers these points). This would have demonstrated that the applicant was familiar with the course content and provided something to talk about at interview.

4. *I am currently taking seven GCSEs including business studies which I enjoy very much. I particularly like learning about the way the financial world works.*

This is better inasmuch as it shows some enthusiasm. However, the applicant:

➡ could have enlarged further on the aspect of the business studies course which he or she enjoyed

➡ could have perhaps related other topics to business studies such as maths if the person is thinking about going into banking. Another example would be any course which involved analytical thinking as business studies would certainly require this. Again, this would be a transferable skill

➡ could have highlighted how any aspects of any of his or her studies had proved valuable on work experience.

5. *My ambition is to be a bank manager or to work for a large finance company.*

Well, I know this is a separate topic as suggested in the *Information for Applicants* leaflet, but do remember that those headings are simply suggestions. This one-liner does nothing to enhance the quality of the application and simply repeats information provided elsewhere.

6. *I enjoy playing netball, and going to the cinema. I also enjoy embroidery and am a keen photographer.*

This is a good start, and the fact that the applicant has time to pursue leisure interests as well as study will be seen positively by the reader. Also, it shows that the applicant has some social and some solitary interests which are quite varied – remember that this shows a 'rounded person'. However, it could be much improved:

- There are two 'enjoy's close to each other. Refer to Chapter 1 for other positive sounding words you can use.

- It might interest the reader to know who the applicant plays netball for. The school? A local team? A national team? Does the applicant have any special responsibilities as part of the team, perhaps organising return matches or refreshments?

- Netball is a team game and a business studies course is sure to involve some team working, probably working on a business project with other students. It would therefore be worth mentioning that you enjoy being part of a team.

- Although it is unlikely that cinema-going will link directly with the college course, the applicant could mention one particular type of film he or she enjoys, for example, thrillers. This is unlikely to help in getting an interview but might give the interviewer something to talk about if they enjoy the same films (never hurts to have something in common with the interviewer).

- Embroidery shows attention to detail, a skill needed in business. A connection could be made here.

- What sort of photography? General? Still life? Birds? People? Sunsets? Like the cinema visits, it may pay to enlarge a little on this section.

7. *I have just passed my First Aid Certificate with the British Red Cross.*

Although this is a non-examined subject it could also have gone under 'Interests', although no harm is done where it is. If I read this though I would wonder why this person chose to do this course. It may be that there is a reason, such as helping in a Brownie pack, which he or she has omitted to mention (you need a lot of leadership skills to run any sort of group).

8.   *I have not yet secured an industrial placement, but have applied to three banks and am awaiting their response.*

This is fine although perhaps a little more detail would help. Which banks? Is the applicant hopeful of the outcome?

There you have it, one 'Further Information' section analysed. Now it's your turn.

Exercise

Read through the 'Further Information' provided below about a student called Jane Smith. She is applying for a BA in Marketing and Psychology at Luton University.

What strengths does the information provided show? How could it be improved?

Further Information
1.   *'As you will see I am applying for course NL57 Marketing and Psychology . I am particular interested in the course that Luton University has to offer because I believe that it contains exactly the mixture of subjects I require to pursue my chosen career in marketing. Additionally, I know that Luton University has a good reputation for this type of course.*

2.   *'Although I now live in London, I was born just outside Luton and it is an area I know well and where I still have many contacts. I feel sure that these factors will help me to settle into the area quickly.*

3. '*In addition to taking psychology A-level, I am also taking English. At this level English is about understanding the characters in the play or book, or identifying the motives behind the writing. I find that my knowledge of psychology has been very helpful here. My third A-level is sociology and the understanding of how society works which I have achieved through the course will be of enormous benefit when learning about marketing and what prompts people to buy a product or service.*

4. '*Unfortunately, I was unable to get an industrial placement working in a marketing company. However, I worked as a receptionist in a hotel where I met a wide variety of people.*

5. '*I enjoy cooking and reading and am a member of the school Debating Society.*'

Don't read any further until you have tried this exercise.

1. '*As you will see I am applying for course NL57 Marketing and Psychology . I am particularly interested in the course that Luton University has to offer because I believe that it contains exactly the mixture of subjects*[i] *I require to pursue my chosen career in Marketing. Additionally, I know that Luton University has a good reputation for this type of course.*[ii]
    i.   This sentence shows that the applicant has really studied the course content and has made a considered judgment.
    ii. A bit of flattery never hurts . . .

2. *Although I now live in London, I was born just outside Luton and it is an area I know well and where I still have many contacts. I feel sure that these factors will help me to settle into the area quickly.*[iii]
    iii. This is a point worth mentioning as selectors will of course want to know that you are really likely to see the course through once you have started it.

3. *In addition to taking psychology A-level, I am also taking English. At this level English is about understanding the characters in the play or book, or identifying the motives behind the writing[iv]. I find that my knowledge of psychology has been very helpful here. My third A-level is sociology and the understanding of how society works which I have achieved through the course will be of enormous benefit when learning about marketing and what prompts people to buy a product or service.[v]*

   iv. This is a nice link between the two subjects. As this application form is not too long, the applicant could perhaps have included an example to highlight the point and to give something to discuss at interview. He or she should certainly be prepared to give examples if asked to do so.

   v. Again, a nice link. Sociology is very relevant to marketing and this sentence shows that the applicant can think his or her way around a number of disciplines and make direct and useful comparisons between them.

4. *Unfortunately, I was unable to get an industrial placement working in a marketing company. However, I worked as a receptionist in a hotel where I met a wide variety of people.[vi]*

   vi. The hotel experience may have offered some valuable points to sell to the reader:

   ◆▸ Did he or she study the way in which the hotel marketed itself? If so, say so, and mention what was learnt.

   ◆▸ What did the type of people who booked into the hotel suggest about how accurately the marketing was targeted? Did the marketing aim at families, single people, business people, holiday makers?

   ◆▸ Was there any valuable experience learnt from dealing with the variety of people?

➥ Did the applicant undertake any special tasks, or do anything 'over and above' that would be worth mentioning?

5. *I enjoy cooking and reading and am a member of the school Debating Society.[vii]*

vii. This is a good mixture of solitary and social pursuits. However, keeping in mind the need to give the interviewer something to talk about perhaps the applicant could have mentioned if there is any particular type of cooking or books hat are enjoyed. Also, being a member of a debating society is likely to have links with at least one of the A-level subjects and perhaps this link could have been made.

Overall, this is a fairly well written section. There is still very little about the type of person the applicant is, although it is implied by the writing. Is he or she energetic, enthusiastic, committed, hard-working, etc? There's no harm in adding a sentence or two – remember the reader is trying to get a sense of you as a person, not just you as a collection of qualifications.

11 Declaration
Don't forget to sign and date the form and remember to send the necessary fee.

What students have to remember is that we read literally dozens of application forms each year. I certainly love to see one that stands out from the crowd in some way. I think "Oh good, this'll be an interesting interview."

Quote from a college lecturer

Chapter Checklist

Have you:

❏ Got the right form? Applicants to universities and colleges of higher education have to complete an UCAS form, applicants for colleges of further education must complete the college's own form. This will be different for each college.

❏ Photocopied the form at least once before you start? Work on the copy so that you don't have to worry about mistakes.

❏ Followed the instructions exactly?

❏ Remembered that the clearing house reduces the size of your application form? Poor writing will be made worse and the reader will struggle.

❏ Presented factual information in a consistent and clear way?

❏ Regarded the 'Further Information' section as a piece of work in its own right? It will need careful preparation and planning.

❏ Remembered that the reader may also be the interviewer? They read many forms and will be pleased to read something a bit out of the ordinary.

❏ Shown that you are really interested in the subject you are applying for?

❏ Mentioned any work or research you have done in your subject area?

❏ Kept a copy of the completed form? You will need to refer to it when you attend an interview.

6 Dazzling CVs

You should read this chapter:

♦♦ when you need to prepare a CV for either a specific job or for a general mailing to a number of organisations.

By the end of this chapter you should know:

♦♦ what a CV is
♦♦ the advantages and disadvantages of this method of presenting information about yourself
♦♦ how to use advertisements, job descriptions and person specifications to help you to construct your CV.

What is a CV?

To get you thinking about the issues around writing a CV here is what the partner of a independent residential resource for young people in need had to say on the subject. He had recently been interviewing for residential workers:

> From a basic point of view I'm looking for writing skills because people have to keep records, etc. I'm also looking for people who have a fair amount of life experience, not necessarily in terms of years, but what they've fitted into those years. I'm looking to see whether they can use very little space to show that they have a good grasp of what the job is, how well thought out their application is and what they can offer the job – rather than that they've just seen the job and salary and thought "I'll have a go at that". In terms of the job description and person specification, I'm checking to see if the essential requirements are met. If the desirable qualities are met too, that's a real bonus.

'I try to use the essential and desirable qualities as a way of being very objective and short-listing on an equal opportunities basis.

'One of the young women in our project was looking for a hairdressing job. She sent off a letter to a lot of local employers which included a lot of CV material. As a result of that she got offered quite a lot of interviews. One of the shops gave her a job. These were people who weren't actually advertising at the time – she got the names from the *Yellow Pages*.

'We'd helped her to word her CV/letter in such a way that it helped to show her personality and allowed the prospective employer to anticipate the sort of person who would be sitting in front of them if they offered her an interview.

'In a time when employers have so much choice of staff to interview, your CV has to stand out in some way. And your personality is one way in which you can stand above the others and stop your details from going in the bin with the others.

'The message to applicants has to be, that interviewers looking to appoint people ask themselves as they read, 'What's so special about you? Why should I interview you? What sort of motivation and investment do you have in the job?" The fact that people feel good about themselves (which is a positive point) should come across on paper.

The term CV is an abbreviation of Curriculum Vitae, which means 'the course of your life'. Having said that, when you are writing a CV, don't take that definition too literally. Employers are not interested in whole chunks of your life, even though they may be fascinating to you. They are only interested in those aspects that demonstrate your skills, qualifications, attitudes and abilities. So, for all practical purposes we could define CV as:

'A history of your work, educational and personal life relevant to the job you are applying for.'

The good (and perhaps bad) news about writing a CV is that there is no single 'correct' way of writing one.

Advantages and disadvantages of the CV

Advantages

- Because there is no single right way to present a CV and because so many people do them poorly, they give you an opportunity to shine over the opposition if you make a good job of yours.
- Unlike application forms *you* decide what to put in your CV.
- Because you choose the CV headings yourself, you can have a separate heading for any unusual work or academic information you wish to present. This is especially useful if you want to emphasise the point rather more than in the little box application forms usually provide for 'Additional Information'. For example, I always have a separate heading for Publications.
- Again, because you choose the headings yourself, you can miss out any information you prefer not to include. This information might include periods of unemployment or poor examination results.
- CV preparation is an excellent way of training your mind to present information succinctly. This may be of real help to you when preparing for an interview.
- The CV is an excellent 'crib sheet' if you are invited to interview.

Disadvantages

- It can feel as if you have to make the whole thing up from scratch each time. Actually, when you have done the work once (by working through this chapter), you will only need to revise it rather than re-write it in future because the bulk of the work will be done.

➧ CVs leave little space for the sort of wider discussion of your abilities you can sometimes write when application forms have that big empty page asking you to provide further information in support of your application.

➧ You really need to use a typewriter or word processor to produce a well presented CV. However, it is much more acceptable to complete an application form by hand, especially as many people have word processors only and it is difficult to ensure the information fits the space allocated on the form.

CV content

Before we go on to the layout of the remainder of the CV we need to consider *what you're actually going to write*. This bit takes plenty of time, although of course you don't have to do it all in one go.

Initially, we'll assume that you are preparing a CV in response to a particular job advertisement, rather than just sending CVs out 'uninvited' (some tips on dealing with 'on spec' CVs will be covered in the next chapter). To do this you need to gather together before you start:

➧ the information you noted about yourself from Chapters 1, 2 and 3

➧ the job advertisement

➧ the job description

➧ the person specification (if one is supplied)

➧ any other information you have about the organisation to which you are applying

➧ plenty of scrap paper (or a new file on your word processor).

Let me take you back a step in case you are not clear about some of the terms.

→ A *job description* describes the job to be done. This usually consists of a list of the main tasks involved in the work. Most employers have a final 'catch-all' heading along the lines of, 'And anything else the manager tells you to do'!

→ A *person specification* describes the person who can do the job. This will be a list of personal and professional attributes the employer seeks for the postholder. It is very common for this list to be split in some way into 'essential' and 'desirable' qualities. When looking through all the application forms the employer will be looking for people who can at least meet all the 'essential' qualities. If there are several or a lot of these, he or she will then seek out those applicants who have as many as possible of the 'desirable' qualities also.

This sounds a bit confusing but, for example, the job description for a typist may include an item which simply says 'type reports'. However, the employer knows it's a busy office and there's a lot of work to get through so the person specification may say, 'able to type at least 45 words per minute'. Another example would be an employer who doesn't actually need a non-smoker because the workplace is not subject to any particular hygiene regulations, but who seeks a non-smoker to comply with company policy.

You may have applied for the job but not have been sent a job description, person specification or any information about the organisation. If so, you need to do some basic detective work. Here is a step by step guide:

→ Phone the organisation and ask (very politely) if they can provide you with any of these documents. If they can't, and you are unclear exactly what the

Angela was determined to find out all she could about the job.

job will entail, ask if you can speak to the
Personnel Manager or whoever is dealing with the
vacancy to obtain more details. Remember when
you do this that you need to sound polished and
confident, because the conversation (as well as
your CV) might affect your chances of an
interview.

♦♦ If this is still not possible, phone your local careers
office or Jobcentre to see if they can give you any
clues. They may not be able to help with the
person specification but will almost certainly be
able to give some ideas about what the type of job
may involve. They are also likely to know
something about most employers in your region,
especially if they have used the employment service
to fill a vacancy.

♦♦ Look for further information about the organisation. This may be:

~ by word of mouth; find out what other people
know about them

~ by keeping an eye on the local press

~ by looking in the national press if it's a big
  organisation
~ by looking in trade or professional journals
  (your main library will probably have them).

From this basic information you can work out for yourself what the person specification is likely to include.
Later in this chapter there are a couple of job descriptions
and person specifications which will give you some idea
of the connection between the two.

Writing a person specification from a job description and advertisement

Of course, you can never be exactly sure of what the person specification might say (for example, you can't know
if you're not told that there is no wheelchair access or that
they're looking for a non-smoker). However, you can
make a reasonably intelligent guess and probably pick up
most of the main points. Here is one example to show
you how to do it. We'll start with the advertisement
which will give you some valuable information.

NIGHT SHIFT WORKER
MACHINE OPERATOR

Tasty Bread Products Ltd are seeking three additional
night shift workers to help produce our high quality
bread products.

Applicants should have good health and be aged between
16 and 45. Full training given although experience of this
type of work would be an advantage.

Basic pay £XX for a 41 hour week, four weeks' annual
holiday.

For details, contact:
Tasty Bread Products Ltd,
Broomfield Road, Manchester, M12 3RR

Now look at the job description:

TASTY BREAD PRODUCTS LTD
JOB DESCRIPTION
MACHINE OPERATOR

Machine operators are accountable to the Production Supervisor, Mr G Smith.

1. Ensure that the correct ingredients are added to machines to guarantee production to the correct standards.
2. Follow the progress of the mixture to the next stage of processing.
3. Check that hygiene standards are followed.
4. Clean the machine at the end of the shift.
5. Make adjustment to the machine as necessary to ensure smooth operation.
6. Report any faults.

Now you've got a wealth of information.

===== **Exercise** =====

Read through the advertisement and job description carefully and underline any words which you think are important. *Do not read any further until this exercise is complete.*

Here are the points that I feel are important.

NIGHT SHIFT WORKER
MACHINE OPERATOR

Tasty Bread Products Ltd are seeking three additional night shift workers to help produce our high quality bread products.

Applicants should have good health and be aged between 16 and 45. Full training given although experience of this type of work would be an advantage.

Basic pay £XX for a 41 hour week, four weeks' annual holiday.

For details, contact:
Tasty Bread Products Ltd
Broomfield Road, Manchester, M12 3RR

JOB DESCRIPTION

1. Ensure that the <u>correct ingredients</u> are added to machines to guarantee bread to the correct standards.
2. Follow the <u>progress</u> of the mixture to the next stage of processing.
3. Check that <u>hygiene standards</u> are followed.
4. <u>Clean</u> the machine at the end of the shift.
5. <u>Make adjustment</u> to the machine as necessary to ensure smooth operation.
6. Report any faults.

Now, what sort of person would they be looking for to do this type of work?

Here are some factors that might well be included in the person specification.

1. The fact that this is the night shift and that the advertisement suggests someone aged between 16 and 45, coupled with the fact that the machine referred to is probably one of those very big food mixing machines, suggests that they need somebody **able bodied** and at least reasonably **fit.**
2. The emphasis on correct ingredients suggest a need for **attention to detail.**
3. The person must be **observant** to ensure that the mixture is progressing satisfactorily (and also to note whether the machinery is operating effectively).
4. The person must be **clean and tidy** to maintain hygiene standards.
5. The person must be **thorough** to clean the machine properly (food manufacturers can incur huge fines if their machinery is dirty, so this is very important).
6. The person must be **able to use their initiative** to

decide whether to try to fix a fault him/herself or to
report it to someone else.

I am sure that this working environment would also be
one where people would not be allowed to smoke.

There you have it. Knowing nothing about food production techniques (as indeed you may not if it's your
first job and you've no prior knowledge), I've made a
reasonably intelligent guess at the contents of the person
specification for a machine operator. So the finished
article might look something like this:

PERSON SPECIFICATION
MACHINE OPERATOR

E = Essential **D = Desirable**

The person appointed to this post must be:

1.	Fit and able-bodied	E
2.	Preferably between 16 – 45	D
3.	Able to prove good attention to detail	E
4.	Observant	E
5.	Clean and tidy	E
6.	Thorough in their approach to work	E
7.	Able to use initiative	E

Now it's your turn.

> I spend a lot of time working
> on an application form, usually
> several hours spread over two or
> three days. It must work – I
> always get invited to interview.

Quote from an employee

Exercise

Below is an advertisement and job description for a training officer. Using the process described above, work out the likely person specification.

STAFF TRAINING OFFICER
Housing and Social Services

We are looking for a suitably qualified graduate to join our small lively team involved in developing our human resource.

Broxbridge has a high commitment to staff development. New legislation, alterations in the structure of the department and changes in working practices mean that we seek an additional training officer to assist in staff training in a wide range of subjects. We seek someone with Human Resource qualifications, and preferably with some training experience.

Send an up to date CV to:

Ms D Jones, Personnel Manager,
Broxbridge Borough Council,
Room 114, Central Block,
High Street, Broxbridge, L11 T56

BROXBRIDGE BOROUGH COUNCIL
STAFF TRAINING OFFICER
JOB DESCRIPTION

Responsible to: *Scale:*
Staff Group Training Manager   Grade C

Main purpose of job
The Staff Training Officer is responsible to the Staff Group Training Manager for assisting Senior Staff Training Officers in the provision of training and development for all members of staff.

Duties:

1. To analyse the training and development needs of individual members of staff and staff groups.
2. To assist in the design and delivery of appropriate training courses and development strategies to meet these needs.
3. To identify training provided out of house and to keep staff informed of such opportunities.
4. To evaluate the effectiveness of training provided both internally and externally.
5. To stock and catalogue a library of resource material for the training department.
6. To undertake any other duties as identified by the Staff Group Training Manager.

How did you get on? Did you consider general issues that you might have known from simply being aware of what's going on around you. For example, the person specification for this particular job is likely to include something about:

- a commitment to equal opportunities and non-discriminatory training
- the candidate being a non-smoker

because these are requirements of many councils. It would make sense therefore to slip these details somewhere in your CV. Even if they are not on the actual person specification they would be welcomed.

Just to remind you – person specifications are usually divided into 'essential' and 'desirable' qualities. If you have to write your own person specification, try to work out which would be which and ensure that you try to prove that you can meet at least the essential requirements.

OK, so now you have all that you need to get down to work. Let's start with the easy bit.

I interviewed one young woman who I felt was really special. She'd taken a year out before college and gone to Australia, then she'd gone to Africa and ended up living in a rural African village where she was the only white woman. She told me her experiences and it was clear she was very mature and had a lot of the skills we would like. I'm so glad I interviewed her, but she hadn't used any of this very relevant experience on her CV so I could easily have missed speaking to her.

Quote from a manager interviewing for a child care worker

Factual details

There are certain facts about you which you should always include on a CV. These are:

- ➥ your full name
- ➥ your full address, including postcode
- ➥ your telephone number, including STD code, or a contact number if you don't have a phone of your own
- ➥ your date of birth.

Health

You don't need to state your health on your CV if you would prefer not to, but you will almost certainly be asked this on an application form. If your health is good, with no problems, state 'excellent' (anything less, even 'good', and people will think there is something wrong!). Chapter

4 discusses in more detail how to present health difficulties that need to be disclosed.

Nationality
Some people also add details of nationality to their CV. There seems little point in using valuable space for this purpose.

Marital status
The choice is open as far as marital status is concerned. Usually it is irrelevant for most vacancies. However, do be sure to state your status if you think it is important. Women may like to be more selective about this because there is still plenty of prejudice.

Here is an example of how to present this basic information:

PHILIPPA RUDONISKY
123 Peterson Road
Walmsley
Lancs, WM2 3ER
0333 67890
Date of birth: 16 June 1973

Note that the words 'Curriculum Vitae' do not appear at the top of the page. There is no rule which says that you have to state this is what the document is – after all, it's fairly obvious. The other common presentation is:

CURRICULUM VITAE

Name: **Philippa Rudonisky**

Address: **123 Peterson Road**
                      Walmsley
                      Lancs
                      WM2 3ER

Telephone: **0333 67890**

Date of birth: **16 June 1973**

Here, name and address are stated even though it's fairly obvious. However, you may like to use this format if it follows the same presentation as information on the rest of the page, eg

Examinations: GCSE English Language

In this case the presentation will be much more uniform and easier on the eye.

Exercise

Decide which way you're going to write your factual details.

> Weirdly enough, quite a lot of people actually put the *time* of their birth as well as the date. Do they think I'm going to do their horoscope to help me decide who to interview?

Quote from an office manager

Selling statement

At the beginning of your CV, immediately below your name and address section, you should write a punchy selling statement. This is a brief statement about yourself that lets the reader have a really powerful idea of the person you are and makes them think, 'Yes! This person I want to see!'

This is where you sell all those intangible aspects of your personality that make you so great to employ. You've already given evidence of them, now's your chance to name them and sell them blatantly. What are they?

In his book, *Hiring the Best*, John Martin Yates lists the 17 personality traits of a successful employee. Here is his list:

Personal traits

Drive: Has a desire to get things done; is goal rather than task oriented; has an ability to make decisions and to avoid busy work; breaks overwhelming tasks into their component parts.

Motivation: Looks for new challenges; has enthusiasm and a willingness to ask questions; can motivate others through their own interests in doing a good job.

Communication: Can talk and write to people at all levels (which, in our information age, is increasingly important).

Chemistry: Does not get rattled and point the finger of blame; wears a smile; has confidence without self-importance; is co-operative with others; demonstrates leadership by an ability to draw a team together.

Energy: Always gives that extra effort in the small things as well as the important matters.

Determination: Does not back off when the going gets tough; has the ability to cope; can be assertive when necessary; is, at the same time, shrewd enough to know when it is time to back off.

Confidence: Is not ostentatious; is poised, friendly, honest with all employees, high and low; yet knows when to keep a secret.

Professional traits

Reliability: Follows up on self; does not rely on others to ensure that a job is well done; keeps management informed.

Integrity: Takes responsibility for own actions, whether good or bad; makes decisions in the best interests of the company, not on whim or personal preference.

Dedication: Has a commitment to tasks and projects; does what is necessary to see a project through to completion on deadline.

Pride: Has pride in trade or profession; takes the extra step and always pays attention to details to see the job is done to the best of ability.

Shaun had worked hard on his selling statement.

Analytical skills: Weighs the pros and cons; does not jump at the first solution that presents itself; analyses the short- and long-term benefits of a solution against all its possible negatives; possesses the perception of a solution against all its possible negatives; possesses the perception and insight that leads to good judgement.

Listening skills: Listens and understands rather than waits for a chance to speak; has attentiveness that complements analytical skills.

Business traits

Efficiency: Always keeps an eye open for wastes of time, effort, resources, and money.

Economy: Knows the difference between expensive and cheap solutions to problems; spends your money as if it were his or her own.

Procedures: Knows that procedures usually exist for good reason, and won't work around them; has a willingness to keep you informed; follows the chain of command; does not implement own 'improved' procedures or organise others to do so.

Profit: Knows it's the reason we're all here.

Daunting list, isn't it? However, I doubt there's many real people who possess all these qualities and most employers are realistic enough to know that. They will, however, be looking for some of them.

=========================== **Exercise** ===========================

Make a list of the personality traits that you think apply to you and what examples you can provide if you get to interview. Keep in mind that much of your evidence will be amply demonstrated by the 'noteworthy extras' you have listed above. However, it is possible that you can give an example from some other area of your CV, such as the interests section.

> One person actually wrote "I think I'm assertive, but my daughter says I'm bossy!" This may have been an amusing thing to say at interview, but it's definitely not the sort of thing to write on an application form or CV.

Quote from a manager

Here is an example of a selling statement prepared by an applicant for the Training Officer job we looked at a while back:

Staff and Management Development Professional. I work well with staff at all levels. Energetic and enthusiastic, I have experience in running a wide range of staff development courses. I am also computer literate, competent on several software packages.

and one for the night shift worker's vacancy:

> Experienced worker with excellent attention to detail. Knowledge of hygiene regulations and food production techniques.

An alternative way of showing 'personality' information

If your selling statement box at the top of your CV is fairly full with factual detail you may wish to tell the reader about your wonderful personality elsewhere. This could come under the heading of 'Other Information'. The next section features other items to include under this heading, but if you choose to use this section to sell your personality make it as punchy and descriptive as you can. As the interviewer at the beginning of this chapter said, let the reader know the sort of person they can expect to see sitting in front of them if they offer you an interview. Here are some examples:

'I am a reliable and enthusiastic worker. I enjoy working with others and can work well without supervision.'

'I am a punctual and dependable person. I am used to working under tight deadlines and enjoy a challenge.'

'I am very enthusiastic about working with computers and have received a lot of positive feedback about my ability to teach software packages to others.'

'I enjoy working with people. I believe I am a good listener and am empathetic to the needs of young children and their parents.'

'Experienced model-maker, excellent at precision work. Good liaison and team-working skills.'

'Enthusiastic trainee mechanic with considerable practical experience.'

'Experienced and enthusiastic group leader, highly committed to helping others work towards a common goal.'

Education and training information

There are actually two headings here – 'Education' and 'Training'. Depending on your own particular circumstances you might chose to separate the information or put them together. Whichever way you choose, here are a few tips that will help you to present the information in the best possible way. That means best for you in getting noticed and best for the reader for ease of understanding:

Education information

Education information consists of three groups of information – where you attended school/college, when, and the qualifications you obtained.

- No employer is likely to be interested in details of your primary school so don't include this information.
- Don't give the whole address of secondary schools or college; simply 'St John's School, Romford' is enough.
- Remember to be consistent in the way you present information.
- If you are writing a 'list' of, say, exam passes, put the ones most connected to the job you are applying for at the top.
- The higher up the educational ladder you go, the less you need mention lower qualifications, so if you:
  - ~ only have five GCSEs mention each one separately. Also, if you are a school-leaver you would normally add the grades you achieved
  - ~ if you have a degree, simply say '5 GCSE passes'; you may like to put the grade of your degree

~ the exception to this rule is if the job you are applying for asks for a particular qualification (for example, some jobs seem to ask for maths GCSE even though you need no higher maths qualifications). Likewise if you think the reader would be interested to know about a particular subject because of its relevance to the job.

You'd be surprised how many people write their whole address under 'Place of Birth'. Anyone would think we need to know that they were born in Flat 2, 27 High Street. Tell people they only need to write the town (and country if out of the UK).

Quote from a personnel manager

Here is an example of how to present education information:

Name:	Jennifer Ann Peters
Address:	26 Sunningdale Road Marlsham Norfolk, NR2 6AS
Telephone:	0990 65656
Date of birth:	26.12.1974
Health:	Excellent

Schools attended:

1986–91	St John's School, High Barns, Cambridge
1991–present	Berne Community College, Marlsham, Norfolk

Education and training:

1991	GCSE			
	English	B	Mathematics	C
	Geography	A	History	C
	Art	A	Sociology	B
	Child Care	C		

1993	GCE A-level English and Sociology (results awaited)

1993	British Red Cross First Aid Basic Certificate

Training information

The term training covers a multitude of different teaching methods:

- short courses
- longer retraining courses that are not certificated
- units of NVQs
- apprenticeships
- in-company courses
- coaching by other staff members
- spending time with staff in different departments to learn what they do
- evening classes.

Any, or all of these, are likely to be of interest to a potential employer. Some people like going on courses and soon collect quite a long list of these. If this applies to you be selective about which ones to include. Don't include courses which have no bearing at all on the job unless you can make a real link. The link, by the way, may be that the course (perhaps recreational) highlights some personal characteristic that will be useful for the work. If so, try to spell this out, perhaps in the 'Additional Information' section, or the reader may not understand the point.

Here are some tips about presenting 'training' information:

- List your courses in the best possible order – by relevance to the job and by standard.
- If the course title leaves the reader unclear as to its content *very briefly* state what was included, perhaps by listing the modules.
- If the course is a long one but still did not lead to a qualification, state the length or the reader may think that you have listed another short course.
- State where you did the course, but don't put the whole address. Simply 'Cambridge Regional College' or 'Timeworks, London' is sufficient.
- Do remember to consider transferable skills when you are deciding which courses to include in your list. For example, suppose you worked in a shop and the company sent you on a 'Customer Care' course. The skills you learn on that course would be just as valuable if you become a sales rep, a customer services manager, work in a different type of shop or indeed anywhere else where you have direct contact with customers.

Exercise

Make a note of your education and training details. Remember to include date, school/college attended, brief address, qualifications and grades (if appropriate) for education; and date, course title, content (if necessary) and organisation for training.

Work experience/Career to date

This section will undoubtedly take you the longest to compose because you should aim to get it exactly right. You will see that I have given this section two headings and you can chose whichever you prefer or indeed make up another as long as it expresses clearly what you want to say.

The prospective employer will read through the education section of your CV, and briefly note if you've got the right qualifications, but this is the section they will scrutinise most closely. Therefore time taken here is well spent.

If you have worked your way through Chapter 1 you will have already undertaken a lot of the work you need to do under this heading. If you haven't, go back now and work through the material so that you have:

- an accurate assessment of *all* your skills
- an idea how to use words to best effect.

Before you consider how to present this information remember that it must be woven into the fabric of your work experience (by work experience I include *all forms of work*). There are a number of different ways to show work experience on a CV and we'll look at those later in this chapter.

Exercise

1. In your notebook, list all your work experience. Don't forget to include holiday jobs, part-time work, full-time work, voluntary work, work experience/ shadowing.
2. Then, under each heading, note your dates – from start of employment to finish (month and year is sufficient).
3. Now take each of the jobs in turn and make a note of the responsibilities you held in that job. These are likely to be much the same as the job description, so if you've kept them that will save you time. Do try to remember though if you gained any additional responsibilities – most jobs develop over time as the needs of the organisation or the interests of the employee shape them.
4. Now for each of those jobs ask yourself 'What did I do that was noteworthy?' These are the special things you noted in Chapter 2.

Here is a tip that could well make your CV stand out from the crowd. When you are writing your 'Work Experience' section you will of course be trying to tie up your experience with what the job description and person specification you have received state. When you select your actual wording, try to weave into your statements those words that you underlined as being significant in those documents. This will work on the reader either consciously or unconsciously and help them to feel well disposed towards your application.

The first thing the interviewer said to me was "We were very impressed by your CV". It helped me to feel good straight away.

Quote from a receptionist

OK, so now you have:

- job titles
- factual details about them – date, etc
- responsibilities in each job
- noteworthy 'extras' for each job.

Strictly speaking, that is all you need for the 'Career to Date' section. More examples of this section of the CV are provided in the next chapter.

Other information

As with the factual information, there is a choice of layout and headings for the odds and ends you still want to get across to the reader but which haven't fitted neatly within any of the previous headings. Most commonly used headings are (1) and (2) overleaf. However, if you do have any additional skills to those listed but which you think might be useful do put them under a separate heading as in (3). Also, mention any work you have had published and, if appropriate, include details of referees.

1. Leisure interests
2. Additional information
3. Additional skills
4. Publications
5. References

One applicant wrote, "As a Christian, I enjoy helping other people, and as a Christian I believe that I would have a lot to offer your sort of work." Altogether this person mentioned being a Christian six times on the application form. There's nothing wrong with being a Christian, of course, but this person came across as if she could think of nothing else. We are a charity but not a religious one, and it seemed inappropriate to give this one aspect of her life such emphasis.

Quote from the manager of a charitable organisation

Leisure interests

It is more or less expected that you will include a section under this heading, although you may choose to use the heading 'Additional Information' if that feels more appropriate (for example, if you want to include both leisure interests and information about one of the items in the next section). For ideas on how to present leisure information turn to page 16.

Additional information

The type of additional information that may well interest a prospective employer (or indeed college) would be:

- membership of a club
- membership of a debating society
- extra responsibilities at school or college (for example, being a prefect)
- involvement with a charity or fund-raising organisation
- playing sports
- voluntary work
- Duke of Edinburgh award.

Having said that, some of these activities may well have provided you with experience that you can emphasise in the body of your CV.

If this isn't the case, don't just list the information. Think instead what it says about you that might interest an employer. Going through the above list I could easily identify:

Membership of a club can indicate that you are a sociable person, or if the club is based around an interest or skill that you are good at whatever that is. Shows that you are not too much of a 'loner'.

Membership of a debating society indicates an ability to present yourself verbally, to think through issues logically and calmly.

Extra responsibilities at school or college (for example, being a prefect) show that you are reliable, trustworthy, respected, etc.

Involvement with a charity or fund-raising organisation shows that you think of others, get involved in things, have initiative.

Playing sports shows that you are fit. Playing a team sport shows that you can work as a member of a team, play by the rules, etc.

Voluntary work shows that you like to help others less fortunate than yourself. Shows reliability, initiative, etc.

Duke of Edinburgh award shows many positive aspects depending on what you've covered. Certainly shows staying power, reliability and willingness to work hard.

Providing this information to prospective employers is especially important if you are a school or college leaver with no work experience to offer as proof of your abilities.

Publications

If you've been fortunate enough to have something published, no matter how modest the publication, do mention it. The format is:

*Name of article   Journal/Publisher   Date of publication
or book*

Generally, the titles of articles are shown in plain type with quotation marks and the title of books are shown in italic type.

If what you have written in any way relates to the job you are applying for, you may want to provide a précis of your article or book as this should interest a prospective employer.

References

It is entirely up to you to decide whether or not to provide details of referees on your CV. If you are applying for a specific job, it is helpful to include this information because some organisations insist on having the reference in front of them prior to the interview.

If, however, you are sending a CV out uninvited (see Chapter 7) there is no need to include this information unless you particularly want to. The organisation can always ask for the details of referees if they contact you for interview.

When you do provide this information choose your referees carefully. You should select people who you feel have a good opinion of you and who know something about you in the capacity you are seeking. Do check with them that they will be willing to provide a reference. It sometimes happens that people get letters requesting a reference on someone they feel is totally unsuitable for the job in question and this can be very embarrassing. Much better to check it out first. If the person agrees to provide a reference, do tell them about the job so that they have a chance to think about it ahead of time.

It is usual to supply the names, addresses and telephone numbers of two referees. Obviously if you have had a previous job, one of your referees should be your previous manager. If you have not had a previous job you could consider asking:

- a teacher from school or lecturer from college
- a professional person who knows you well
- the chairperson or leader of a club you belong to
- a family friend who has a professional job.

Do check with these people first that they are willing to write a reference for you. Also, if you are applying for a specific vacancy, find out if they are away on holiday at the time their reference will be needed.

If you are already employed and do not want your present employer to know that you are applying for other jobs, mention this in your covering letter (some application forms ask the question anyway). Simply say something like 'Please do not contact my employer for a reference unless a job offer is to be made'.

Chapter Checklist

In this chapter we have looked at two areas:

1. presenting factual information, and
2. presenting additional information.

Some points to consider are:

❏ always give yourself plenty of time to prepare a CV

❏ gather all the information you need before you start

❏ study all the information available about the job and organisation

❏ underline/highlight those words that are most important

❏ always start by thinking about what the employer is looking for

❏ mould your answer to the employer's stated needs (or what you think they are)

❏ use lots of positive words

❏ really sell your successes

❏ remember to sell yourself as a 'balanced' person

❏ if no suitable job openings appear, consider sending out your CV 'on spec' (further details in the next chapter).

7 CV Layouts

You should read this chapter:

➥ when you have gathered together all the information you wish to include in a CV.

By the end of this chapter you should know:

➥ the variety of ways in which a CV can be presented
➥ the advantages and disadvantages of each format
➥ which format will best suit your purpose
➥ what steps to take if you decide to send out your CV 'speculatively'.

CV choices

In Chapter 6 we looked at the different ways to present factual information. There are some quite fundamentally different layouts you could consider to present information in your CV. Each has its advantages and disadvantages. Let's look at some.

Chronological CV

As the name suggests, a chronological CV presents material in chronological (date) order *in reverse* – that is, most recent information is shown first. The chronological CV takes the reader step by step through your education history, then your experience history and finally to your additional information.

The advantages of the chronological CV are:

➥ it is the one most employers are familiar with
➥ employers can find out a lot about you if they read this type of CV carefully – information such as

whether you have any career gaps, etc

♦♦ it fills up a page if you are young and don't yet have much experience to offer

♦♦ it provides a useful reference guide to you for future CVs and indeed application forms.

The disadvantages are:

♦♦ it can be a fairly bland predictable read for a prospective interviewer.

In graphic form, the chronological CV looks like this:

Name

Address

Telephone

Date of birth

Selling statement

Education and training
Dates, names of schools, details of exams

Career to date
Dates, name and address of employer
Job titles, responsibilities
Any 'extras' you can claim

Additional information

Even within this format though, there is a choice of how to present information. Remember, there are several ways to do this, choose whichever you prefer. The golden rule is MAKE IT EASY FOR THE READER TO ABSORB THE INFORMATION YOU PROVIDE. This means presenting your information attractively and consistently.

Having said that, there is one 'wrong' way to write a CV and that is to mix styles. Look at this example:

CURRICULUM VITAE

Name: Philippa Rudonisky

Address: 123 Peterson Road,
                 Walmsley,
                 Lancs,
                 WM2 3ER

Telephone: 0333 67890

Date of birth: 16 June 1973

Education and Training

Sept 1984–   Collett Community College, Gilbert Road,
July 1989   Walmsley

                 Examinations: GCSE
                 English   C
                 Maths   D
                 Textiles   C
                 Business Studies   C
                 Geography   D

Sept 1989   Walmsley Regional College, Bailey Road,
                 Walmsley

July 1990   City and Guilds General Catering

                 Accommodation services and reception –
                 written

                 Accommodation services and Reception –
                 practical

July 1990   Royal Inst of Public Health and Hygiene –
                 Credit

Sept 1990–   Walmsley Regional College, Bailey Road,
July 1992   Walmsley
                 BTEC National Diploma in Social Care.

2.9.1993   Walmsley Regional College, Bailey Road
to present   RSA Business Administration

Work Experience
Part-time work, while at college or school:

N.A.S. Newsagents, Victoria Lane, Walmsley
July 1987–February 1989
Saturday position involving handling money, dealing with
customers, sorting out paper bills, and shelf filing.

Bakers Food Shops, Arthur Street, Walmsley 3.3.89–3.9.90
This job involved handling money, helping customers, filling
shelves and working as part of a team.

Jane Pearce Elderly People's Home, Fortescue Road, Walmsley
Sept 1990–June 1992
I worked at Jane Pearce House in the kitchens as a weekend
cook to support me through college. This involved the ability
to supervise others, devise and cook menus as well as prepare
the evening tea.

Full-time work since leaving college
Jane Pearce Elderly People's Home, Fortescue Road, Walmsley
July 1993–September 1993
Care Assistant. This responsible role involved caring for elder-
ly people, ambulance escort duty, collecting and banking
money and the supervision of others.

Other Information
I enjoy working and being with others. I also enjoy swimming,
needlepoint and dancing. I am a keen cook and like to
experiment in the kitchen. I am a student associate member of
The Institute of Qualified Private Secretaries.

Can you spot the deliberate mistakes?

- Inconsistent method of presenting dates, eg 2.9.92
  and July 1989 – make sure you use the same system
  throughout.
- Inconsistent way of showing an address (part
  missed off on one line).
- On one line 'reception' starts with a capital letter,
  on another it doesn't.
- Spelling mistake – 'filing' not 'filling'.
- Inconsistent use of underlining and bold to
  emphasise words.

•→ Not all the jobs show the job title even though it is implied by the type of work undertaken. They should always be shown and always displayed in a similar manner to the others.

Skills based (or functional) CV

As the name suggests this CV presentation is written to emphasise skills rather than take the reader chronologically through the life of the writer. This is an increasingly popular form of CV presentation, although it does require that you already have relevant skills or you'll find it difficult to fill a page!

To write a skills based CV you simply do the same preparation as before, linking your skills with the job requirements. Then you present your skills in a punchy and eye-catching way.

Below the skills is a very brief summary of your work experience and education. As you will see from the examples which follow, this type of CV does not state which skills have been used in which job.

A skills based CV often fits on one side of A4 paper.

Here are some graphic examples of this type of CV:

Name
Address
Telephone
Date of birth

Selling statement

Education
Brief details only

Capabilities
•→ list them here using bullet points

Achievements
•→ again, list them here using bullet points

Work History (or 'Career to Date')
➤ for each job list brief details of:
Employer's name and short address
Dates of employment
Job title

Additional Information
Unless you decide to provide this information in your covering letter

Or alternatively:

Name
Address
Telephone
Date of birth

Education
Brief details only

One Skill Area
➤ list skills under this heading using bullet points

Another Skill Area
➤ as before, list skills using bullet points

Continue until you run out of skills

Work History (or 'Career to Date')
➤ for each job list brief details of:
Employer's name and short address
Dates of employment
Job title

Additional Information
Unless you decide to provide this information in your covering letter

Collette's chronological CV

I'm assuming for this CV that Collette is looking a secretarial job and is sending her CV out 'on spec' to a number of local companies. Note that she has stated at the top of the CV the type of work she is looking for. She would, of course, also mention this in her covering letter.

Name	Collette Hay
Address	27 Blinco Road Wareham Lancs
Telephone	0333 787870
Date of birth	16.12.1976

Job target: Administrative or secretarial post

A conscientious and hardworking school leaver with up to date secretarial skills

Work experience

May 1993– June 1993	Hurst's Office Supplies Ltd High Street, Wareham Admin Assistant

- typing letters and invoices
- filing
- answering the telephone
- relief reception work

Vacation work

July 1993– Sept 1993	St Joseph's Home Dear Street, Wareham Day Care Assistant

- working with a variety of professionals
- dealing with a variety of personal needs of the residents
- writing diary notes on each resident
- dealing with the relatives of residents
- taking part in outings, etc

Whilst working at St Joseph's I invented a new board game for the residents which has proved very popular.

Education
1960–1976   St Joseph's Comprehensive, Dear Street,
             Wareham

             GCSE
             English   B
             Mathematics   A
             Geography   C
             History   E
             Child Care   C
             Business Studies   B

             RSA Stage I
             Typewriting

Additional information
For the past two years I have been secretary of the school
drama club. This has given me a wide range of secretarial
experience from taking minutes of meetings to handling
monies from ticket sales. I enjoyed working as part of the team
developing each drama production and also enjoyed working
alone on those aspects of my role which required this.

I am a keen photographer and also enjoy netball and
swimming. I am an enthusiastic reader of historical novels.

References
Mrs Jane Briggs   Mr John Oman
661 Long Road   7 Aubray Road
Wareham   Wareham
Lancs   Lancs

How do you think Collette comes across? She is clearly a
lively and enterprising person who enjoys being with
others. She has a good range of exam passes relevant to
the work she seeks. Additionally, she has managed to pass
these whilst still taking on the work with the drama
group and following her other hobbies. Most employers
with a suitable vacancy would think that she is a person
worth seeing after reading this CV. Added to that, she has

shown considerable initiative in sending it out 'on spec' in the first place. Now we'll see how the CV looks with another format.

Collette's skills based CV

Collette Hay
27 Blinco Road
Wareham
Lancs

0333 787870

16.12.1976

Job target: Administrative or secretarial post

Abilities
◆▸ typing letters and invoices
◆▸ filing
◆▸ answering the telephone
◆▸ reception work
◆▸ message-taking
◆▸ working with people at all levels

Work experience
July 1993–Sept 1993	St Joseph's Home Dear Street, Wareham *Day Care Assistant*
May 1993–June 1993	Hurst's Office Supplies Ltd High Street, Wareham *Admin Assistant*

Qualifications
◆▸ 6 GCSEs including English and Business Studies
◆▸ RSA Typewriting Stage I

Additional Information
I am a conscientious and hardworking person who enjoys working as part of a team but am also well motivated to work unsupervised. I pay good attention to detail and enjoy working to deadlines.

I am a keen photographer and also enjoy netball and swimming. I am an enthusiastic reader of historical novels.

Put yourself in the shoes of the person short-listing candidates for a job. She or he is looking for people who can meet those criteria outlined on the job description and person specification. The skills based CV does save time checking skills because they don't have to be picked out one at a time from the variety of jobs the applicant has shown.

Juliette's skills were easy to identify.

Spacing

As we've seen earlier, one rule on CV presentation is that you don't use more than two sides of A4. As a school leaver, you may find it difficult to fill two sides. Collette's skills based CV, when presented on A4 paper, might fill only one side. If it just goes over on to the second page, she would have to make a decision either to space out the work so that it fills the second page, or to squash it up a bit to get it on one page.

Don't worry if the whole of page two isn't full, but try to write on a least two-thirds of it. To 'squeeze' or 'expand' your information you can:

- have bigger or smaller margins
- leave more or less space between each heading
- list examination results under each other or side by side (don't simply say '6 GCSE passes' if these are your only qualifications)
- write any addresses over one or more lines
- put the referee information side by side or under each other.

Think carefully before cramming a lot of information on one page to make it fit. Crowded pages are not nearly so attractive to the eye as those with lots of 'white space'.

CV for a second job

James wants to apply for a job as trainee manager with a nationwide white goods store.

James's chronological CV

CURRICULUM VITAE

James Matthew Whiteways

27 High Meadows, Thornton, Glasgow, GL3 1AH

0234 343536

1.2.1976

Health: Excellent

An enthusiastic and successful retail salesman with experience of selling electrical equipment and stock control systems.

Education and training

1987–1992	Wells Community College, Walmersley, Glasgow		
	GCSE	English	Grade B
		Maths	Grade C
		Art	Grade C
		History	Grade E
		Geography	Grade D
		French	Grade E

1992	Hodder Electrical In-Service Training Course:
	'Techniques of Selling: Stage 1' – 2 day course
	'Techniques of Selling: Stage 2' – 2 day course
1993	'Controlling Stock' – half day course

Career to date

1992–present	Hodder Electrical Ltd, Highgate Shopping Centre, Glasgow
	Salesman
	Specialist knowledge of stereo systems and video recorders and cameras.
	Responsibility for stock control when manager away.

During the past year I have increased sales in the stereo and video department by 15%.

Vacation experience

1991–92	Campbell's Shoes Ltd, Twenty Street, Glasgow
	Salesman (Saturdays and vacations)
1990–91	The Corner Shop, 23 Garden Road, Thornton, Glasgow
	Newspaper Delivery Boy

Interests

I am an enthusiastic footballer and a member of Thornton Sports and Social Club Committee where I have responsibility for social activities. I enjoy reading thrillers and socialising with friends.

This isn't a bad CV, but as James is applying for his second job he'd have done better to put the 'Career to Date' section before 'Education and Training' even though he has done some useful courses whilst working at Hodder Electrical. He has wisely remembered to include something he has done that is over and above the normal expected of him – he increased sales by 15% in a year.

James's skills based CV

CURRICULUM VITAE

James Matthew Whiteways
27 High Meadows, Thornton,
Glasgow, GL3 1AH

0234 343536
1.2.1976
Health: Excellent

Capabilities

◆◆ Knowledge of white goods of all sorts
◆◆ Specialist knowledge of video and stereo systems and cameras
◆◆ Managing stock control systems
◆◆ Working to target
◆◆ Excellent customer care
◆◆ Working knowledge of word processing

Accomplishments

◆◆ Increased sales in video and stereo department by 15% in one year

Work experience

1992–present   Hodder Electrical Ltd, Highgate Shopping Centre, Glasgow
Salesman

1991–92   Campbell's Shoes Ltd, Twenty Street, Glasgow
Salesman (Saturdays and vacations)

1990–91   The Corner Shop, 23 Garden Road, Thornton, Glasgow
Newspaper Delivery Boy

Education and Training

◆◆ 6 GCSEs including English and Maths

Hodder Electrical In-Service Training Courses

◆◆ 'Techniques of Selling – Stages 1 and 2'
◆◆ 'Controlling Stock'

Additional information

I am a highly motivated and successful salesman who enjoys working as part of a team. I am presentable and relate well to customers. I find that staff often turn to me for advice on a variety of matters.

I am an enthusiastic footballer and a member of Thornton Sports and Social Club Committee where I have responsibility for social activities. I enjoy reading thrillers and socialising with friends.

James's skills based CV does not have the 'selling box' under his basic information as does the chronological CV, although he could have chosen to include the box. He has, however, shown the information under his final section and has wisely mentioned that staff turn to him for advice – useful in view of the job he's applying for. He's also remembered to add that he can use a word processing package.

CV for a graduate with some work experience

Sally, a graduate with work experience, is applying for a job as a researcher with a pressure group working for reform of the prison system.

Sally Jane Dowling
27 Upper North Street
Dainow
DN23 6PB

0229 767676

22.10.1971

Health: Excellent

An energetic and enthusiastic researcher with experience of work in penal reform.

Education

1990–94   BA (Hons) Social Research 2:1
                 University of North London

1982–89   Dainow Comprehensive College
                 Fisher Street, Dainow
                 GCE A-level:
                 Sociology   A
                 English   B
                 History   D

                 GCSE:
                 English, Mathematics, History, Sociology,
                 Geography, Religious Studies, Art

Career to date

1989–90   North East London Probation Service
                 Probation Assistant

                 ◆◆ interviewing probationers
                 ◆◆ writing reports
                 ◆◆ co-leading groups
                 ◆◆ liaising with other professionals
                 ◆◆ attending case conferences

1986–89   Dainow Shoe Company
                 Saturday Sales Assistant

                 ◆◆ serving customers
                 ◆◆ answering telephone

Additional information

I have a long-term interest in the field of criminology and
penal reform. My dissertation at university was on 'Problems
faced by prisoners' families' and won the Jane McDonald
Award for best dissertation of the year in this subject.

I very much enjoyed the research element of my degree which
lasted two years and feel enthusiastic about pursuing penal
reform as a career.

I am a friendly outgoing person and have a passion for
computing. I enjoy working as part of a team, but am well
motivated to work on my own.

Leisure interests

I am a bit of a film buff and enjoy old movies as well as current
releases. I belong to a squash club where I play regularly. I love
reading, especially family novels and suspense.

Here's a skills based version of the same CV:

Sally Jane Dowling
27 Upper North Street
Dainow
DN23 6PB

0229 767676

22.10.1971

Health: Excellent

An energetic and enthusiastic researcher with experience of work in penal reform.

EDUCATION
1994 BA (Hons) 2:1 University of North London

CAPABILITIES
Research

- Problems faced by prisoners' families; qualitative research
- Evaluation of effectiveness of groups in probation
- Two years' study of research methods in BA

Writing

- Writing up research findings
- Writing reports
- Writing diary records of group and case work

Communicating

- Liaising with a wide range of professionals
- Attending case conferences
- Dealing with a variety of clients
- Working as part of a probation team

Computing

- 'Word' word processing
- SSAS research package
- Pagemaker Desk Top Publishing

ACHIEVEMENTS

◆◆ Won the Jane McDonald Award for best dissertation of my year

CAREER TO DATE

1989-90   North East London Probation Service
                Probation Assistant

1986-89   Dainow Shoe Company
                Saturday Sales Assistant

ADDITIONAL INFORMATION

I have a long-term interest in the field of criminology and penal reform. I very much enjoyed the research element of my degree which lasted two years and feel enthusiastic about pursuing penal reform as a career.

I am a friendly outgoing person. I enjoy working as part of a team, but am well motivated to work on my own.

LEISURE INTERESTS

I am a bit of a film buff and enjoy old movies as well as current releases. I belong to a squash club where I play regularly. I love reading, especially family novels and suspense.

In this version Sally may have chosen to leave out the 'Additional Information' and to include it in her covering letter instead. The fact that Sally had won an award for an outstanding dissertation as an undergraduate would be of great interest to a prospective employer. It is well worth, therefore, including it under a heading of 'Achievements'.

If you choose a skills based format for your CV this could be where you provide information on those things you have done that are over and above what is normally expected at work or college.

Spend a few minutes studying the two versions to see their differences. Which would suit your purpose most effectively?

Writing a CV to send out speculatively

So far we have been talking about CVs that are written specifically to apply for a particular job. You may decide that you want to send your CV to several organisations 'on spec'.

Many people hesitate to do this, but what have you got to lose? Only your time and the cost of the stationery and stamps. Remember, if an organisation can fill a vacancy without having to advertise, shortlist and so on, it saves them time and money and a lot of effort.

There are three approaches to sending out CVs speculatively:

1. You send your CV to every organisation you can think of that might have a vacancy. This would work, for example, for a typist job – almost every organisation has some office staff.
2. You send your CV to the types of organisations that may possibly have specific types of work. For example, all building companies in the area if you're looking for a bricklaying job.
3. You send out your CV to organisations that have been in the news and that you think may therefore have an opening in future. This would be the case, for example, if you read that a company had won a big contract, is expanding, has received an award. Anything positive, in fact, might be worth following with a CV and covering letter. Chapter 9 gives information on how to write a covering letter in these circumstances.

Perhaps you are looking for a specific type of work, for example, as a hotel receptionist. No such jobs have been advertised recently in your area. Use your initiative and write yourself a CV as if there were such a job. Send your CV with a covering letter to all the hotels in your area.

The advantages of sending a CV on spec are:

- it shows the organisation that you are self-motivated and can use your initiative
- even if there is not a vacancy at the moment, your information may be kept on file and the

organisation will contact you if a vacancy arises

•• you may catch the organisation at a time when they have just heard of a vacancy and not yet had an opportunity to advertise

•• you may contact the organisation when they are considering starting a new post – you'll be first in the queue

•• you could even find yourself being the only one interviewed because the organisation has not advertised the vacancy, which means that as long as you're good you don't have to worry about other interviewees who might be even better . . .

To sum up:

•• think about the sort of work you want to apply for

•• work out what the job entails and try to write your own job description and person specification

•• write your CV as if you were writing to the organisation for that job

•• write a suitable covering letter, indicating exactly the type of work you seek, or saying that you are open to suggestions. Alternatively, you could say that you are really looking for X job but would be willing to consider others

•• find out the name of the personnel or relevant manager and send your letter and CV direct to that person (again, this shows initiative and will only cost a phone call)

•• consider following up your mailing with a phone call a few days later. If you do this, prepare before-hand for the call: what are you going to say? Make a few notes if you think you will get flustered.

Exercise

Investigate all the organisations in your area (or the area in which you would like to live) who would have the type of vacancy you are looking for. Don't forget to find out to whom CVs should be sent.

FURTHER CV TIPS

DO:

- ➡ be consistent in the way you present material – make it easy for the reader

- ➡ decide which CV style would best present the information you want to show

- ➡ make yourself come alive as a person rather than just a list of facts

- ➡ keep a copy of your CV for future reference

- ➡ consider sending out a CV speculatively, especially if there are few vacancies being advertised in the type of work you seek.

DON'T:

- ➡ use more than two sheets of A4 paper

- ➡ write on the back of the sheet

- ➡ use poor quality paper

- ➡ use abbreviations, especially if they might be unfamiliar to the reader

- ➡ use only one CV for everything. Write a fresh version for each different job. Usually you will only have to make modifications, and not have to do a complete re-write

- ➡ forget what you've written. Use your CV as a crib sheet prior to interview

- ➡ assume that the reader will know about what your past jobs involved

- ➡ forget which version of your CV you've sent. Make a note on your copy of each CV.

Chapter Checklist

In this chapter we have looked at two styles of CV:

1. chronological and
2. skills based.

All CVs include:

❏ Name

❏ Address

❏ Telephone number

❏ Date of birth

❏ Education and training

❏ Work experience (or 'Career to date')

❏ Additional information (or 'Leisure interests')

Other information you may choose to display on your CV include:

❏ Nationality

❏ Health

❏ Marital status

❏ Whether you hold a driving licence

CVs can be sent out:

❏ In response to a particular job advertised

❏ Speculatively in the hope that a vacancy might occur which has not yet been advertised.

8 Job Application Forms

You should read this chapter:

➜➜ before you begin to work on a job application form.

By the end of this chapter you should know:

➜➜ how to use your self-analysis
➜➜ how to present information about yourself
➜➜ how to use job descriptions and person specifications to shape your answers
➜➜ how to show evidence of success.

Matching your application to the job

 I advertised for an Aviation Bird Controller. The job is to try to keep birds away from flight paths at airports by manipulating the environment and other non-violent methods.

In response to the question "Why do you think you're suited to this job?", one person wrote, "I like to kill all things, pidjins and vermin." Awful!

This guy was not very literate and had obviously shown his application form to a friend who

was not much better. The friend
had used a different colour pen and
added some of his own comments
in very distinctively different
handwriting (which was almost
as bad as the applicant's).

Quote from Aviation Bird Control Manager

Guess who didn't even get an interview?

The quote above just had to go at the beginning of the chapter because it's such an extreme (and true) example of what not to write. By working through this chapter you can ensure that your application form avoids errors of any sort.

There are advantages to completing application forms:

- the format is prepared for you, you simply have to fill in the spaces
- sometimes the space provided suggests how much you should write
- the form tells you what information to provide, as well as the format.

Some disadvantages are:

- you may have little flexibility to express yourself
- it is difficult to complete an application form using a word processor
- some organisations use the same form for applicants for all their jobs and so it may be difficult to provide the information you want to get across
- some forms have the dreaded 'tell me why you want the job' box – usually the biggest box.

In fact, application forms vary quite a lot because

different organisations will want to know different things, as you'll see from a couple of real-life examples later in this chapter. However, there are similarities. Almost all forms ask first the familiar questions about name, address, etc. Some organisations that are deeply committed to equal opportunities may not ask for your first name, simply an initial. This is to avoid gender bias. They will probably also ask questions about your ethnic background and any disabilities. This latter information is to help organisations ensure that they are achieving their goals of a more balanced workforce.

As you plan how to complete your application form you need to match what you say about yourself to the job description and person specification as well as to anything you know about the organisation. You also need to work out what you can offer the job and the organisation, why you want the job and why you're applying for the job now. Try to get inside the reader's head. Try to work out what they are looking for and how you can show that you have it (or at least some of it).

Joe could see a picture of his interviewer beginning to form.

With this preparation in mind you are almost ready to start on the form. But two things first. Photocopy it – no smudges, coffee stains or scribbles allowed. Then *read the instructions on the form twice.*

 We ask for people to complete the application form in their own handwriting (that is emphasised on the form) and I feel really irritated when people type it or write in block letters. The job involves some log-keeping and I have to read the logs – I hate having to struggle to read bad handwriting.

Quote from a manager

Most forms are very straightforward and many now make a point of asking questions in clear language (as with the Royal Mail form in this chapter). Nevertheless, the number of forms received with crossings out is amazing.

By using a couple of very different application forms, we'll look at how to present all this information about yourself as effectively as possible. Although advice is focused on these forms, the points would apply to other forms you may have to complete.

One important point. Do read the forms very carefully indeed. The Royal Mail form, for example, gives a lot of instructions and it would be very easy to skip some of them and get it wrong. By working on a photocopy of the original you can check and double-check to ensure that you have missed nothing without fear of spoiling the original.

Application form from a large organisation

Application for a job

We're delighted that you want to join Royal Mail. We'd like you to know that we positively encourage equal opportunities. We'll respect and keep in confidence all the information you give us.

The job

Please write in black ink so that we can make photocopies of this form.

you have applied to join us as

We use this form to draw up a short-list of applicants to interview. We suggest you first read it through thoroughly and then answer it as carefully and as completely as you can.

If you wish to answer any question at greater length, just attach your written answer on a separate sheet. But be sure to write your name on the top!

About yourself

title (Mr, Ms etc.)

your first name

your surname

previous surname(s) *(if you've had any)*

your day-time telephone number

your address

your National Insurance number

postcode

your present nationality

your place of birth

your date of birth

19

Your formal education

We would like you to tell us which schools and colleges you have studied at since you were 11.

name of school or college	from/to	qualifications worked for *(and results)*

This Royal Mail form is worded in a very friendly and encouraging way. Note the comments at the very top about equal opportunities and confidentiality.

The job
Note here that you are asked to write in black ink – do so! Make sure that you use exactly the same job title as you saw in the advertisement or job description.

Note also that you are told that you can write on a separate sheet as long as you write your name on the top of that too.

About yourself
Easy section, but read it through before completion. It's very easy to write the first name in the surname box and vice versa. Don't forget to include your postcode! For 'place of birth' they don't want the whole address, simply the town and county, or town and country if outside the UK.

Your formal education
This form actually instructs you to ignore primary school details, although this is not information that you would normally put on any application form.

- ◆◆ Note that you are only asked for the name of the school or college, not the whole address.
- ◆◆ Write the date details ('from/to') consistently – don't mix, for example 3 March 1988 with 3.3.88. This particular form leaves only a narrow space for the dates so the numbered version would obviously fit more easily anyway. You don't actually need to put the day on which you started or left – the month and year is sufficient.
- ◆◆ You are asked for details of qualifications worked for (and results). This indicates that Royal Mail want to know about exams you have failed as well as those you have passed. The fact that you studied a subject to examination level shows that you

probably know quite a lot about it even if you failed. Again, be consistent with your presentation of these facts – make reading the form as easy as possible for the prospective interviewer. Not all organisations will want to know about exams you failed – in that case you should decide whether to include this information or not.

Your present and previous jobs

Helpful instructions here – *'We would like you to tell us about your present job (where applicable) and any previous jobs you may have had'* and *'Don't forget about any part-time or vacation work, periods when you were not working (tell us what you were doing), periods of unemployment (give us the address of your Benefit Office), time spent in the armed services or any voluntary/community work.'*

Some of these instructions are fairly unusual on application forms – you are not often asked so directly about periods of unemployment, or periods not working. One of the ways in which you can 'disguise' short periods of unemployment is by 'losing' them between dates. For example, if you were unemployed from May to August 1992, you simply don't put the months on the application form. So one job ended in 1992 and the other started the same year with no apparent gaps.

However, to do this when you are so specifically asked to state periods of unemployment, etc would effectively constitute a lie and could lead to dismissal if you were offered the job. For this reason, I would not recommend 'losing' any periods of unemployment on a form like this – own up.

You are asked for:

- part-time work
- vacation work
- periods not working
- periods of unemployment
- time in the forces
- voluntary/community work.

Your present and previous jobs

We would like you to tell us about your present job (where applicable) and any previous jobs you may have had.

Don't forget about any part-time or vacation work, periods when you were not working (tell us what you were doing), periods of unemployment (give us the address of your Benefit Office), time spent in the armed services or any voluntary/community work.

from/to	your employer's name and address	the type of work or position you held	why you left

May we contact your present employer for a reference?

☐ yes, you may   ☐ no, you may not   ☐ it doesn't apply

Have you ever applied for a job in the Post Office before *(this includes Christmas work)*?

☐ no, I haven't   ☐ yes, I have once   ☐ yes, I have more than once

the most recent job I applied for was   at (*which office*)   on

☐   ☐   ☐ 19

I was employed from/to   when I left, my job title was

☐   ☐

To this list I would add industrial or work placements.

This form unfortunately gives you no space to enlarge on the type of work you undertook or how it relates to the job you are applying for. You may well think it worthwhile to get round this by writing on an extra sheet to give this information. Remember, the organisation may literally get hundreds of application forms for each job so yours has to be one better than the rest.

So working first on some spare paper write down the details of all these jobs in date order. Give the most recent first and work backwards. In Chapter 1 you were shown how to analyse your previous experience and relate it to the job you are applying for. In this way you will be able to identify all those positive points about yourself which will interest the prospective interviewer.

Looking at this section in more detail:

From/to

    ➻ As before be consistent with how you present dates.

Your employer's name and address

    ➻ If your old employer's address was very long abbreviate it a bit as there's not much space. Be consistent with presentation.

The type of work or position you held

Keep in mind all those different types of work you were asked to include. This means you not only include job titles, but you have to state why you weren't working at any time if this is the case. If it was for some reason other than unemployment say so – 'illness', 'travelling around the world', 'having a baby'.

In fact, this is the section where you are likely to have to use an additional sheet of paper. If you do so and want to highlight points about several different jobs/periods of unemployment, then signal them to the reader by putting an asterisk (*) against those items. Then put an (*) at the bottom of this column and write next to it, 'See additional sheet'.

If you had periods of unemployment did you do anything unusual or creative with the time? If so, do mention this as it will be of interest to a prospective employer.

Why you left
There are a few unwritten golden rules about explaining why you left a job. Here they are:

- Always try to make the reason for leaving positive rather than negative. Something you wanted to go to, rather than something you wanted to get away from.
- Try to avoid saying you were sacked if you can, but don't tell a lie.
- Don't say something like, ' Because I didn't get on with the boss' – the reader will not know this person and may wonder if you are a trouble-maker.
- Employers like to see that people have moved on for logical reasons – for promotion, to widen skills and experience, because you have moved from one part of the country to another, to get back into education.
- Mentioning redundancy can be OK, although sometimes employers may wonder why you were chosen to be made redundant. If this was because the company or the department closed down then say so, rather than simply 'made redundant'.

May we contact your present employer now for a reference?
If you are currently employed, you may not want your present employer to know you are applying for another job. If so, tick the 'no' box.

Have you ever applied for a job in the Post Office before?

You are only likely to be asked this type of question by very large organisations. The section is fairly self-explanatory.

More about yourself

What do you like doing in your spare time?

_____

_____

_____

_____

Can you ride a bike confidently in bad weather or heavy traffic?

☐ no, I can't   ☐ yes, I can

Have you a full driving licence?

☐ no, I haven't   ☐ yes, I have

Your health

Have you ever had any trouble with your joints, back, neck or knees?

☐ no, I haven't   ☐ yes, I have

it was in/since	details of the problem are
19	

Have you needed to consult a doctor or specialist about an illness in the last year?

☐ no, I haven't   ☐ yes, I have

it was in	details of the illness are
19	

Are you taking any medication prescribed by a doctor (_either regularly or when you need it_)?

☐ no, I am not   ☐ yes, I am

it has been since	I'm taking
19	

Please list all the times you have been absent from your job/from school in the last year (_give dates if possible_).

how many days	when	why

More about yourself

This section initially asks you what you like to do in your spare time. Again, if you have worked through the exercises in Chapter 1 you will have already worked out how best to sell your leisure interests.

 I am an outgoing person who the majority of people find very easy to talk to and it takes a lot for the smile to disappear from my face.

Quote from an application form

Can you ride a bike confidently in bad weather or heavy traffic?

Although this question is fairly specific to working for Royal Mail, you may well see similar job-specific questions on other forms. For example, pizza delivery people would need to ride a motor bike in heavy traffic. Some jobs may require excellent health, or the ability to carry heavy weights. Others may need particular experience such as fluency in a certain language.

Have you a full driving licence?

This is often asked, even for jobs where it doesn't seem immediately relevant.

Your health

These questions are not unusual with work that involves putting your body under some strain. No employer would want to take on someone who is obviously going to take a lot of time off sick. However, answering 'yes' would not immediately exclude you, especially if your health problem has now been overcome.

It is also not unusual to be asked about days off sick, although this is often done at interview. All employers know that there are some people who are, quite frankly, skivers, whilst others genuinely need time off because of poor health. Either way, this will affect the work employers can expect someone to do in a year.

Your record in the community

Have you a criminal record?

☐ no, I haven't ☐ yes, I have, the details are

By 'criminal record' we mean any offence that you were found guilty of committing by Court or Court Martial *(this includes motoring offences).* We also mean any cases that may be pending. Answering yes doesn't mean that we can't consider you for the job. However, we may look more favourably on your application if you give us details of the circumstances.

If you have a conviction that is spent, under the terms of the 'Rehabilitation of Offenders Act 1974 and 1986', you can honestly answer that you don't have a criminal record.

the nature of the offence

[ ]

the sentence or court order

[ ]

the date of conviction

[19]

Have you ever been the subject of bankruptcy proceedings?

☐ no, I haven't ☐ yes, I have

the court where the case was heard

[ ]

Equal opportunities

Royal Mail is very concerned to treat all applicants equally. We don't mean these questions to be intrusive — the information helps us to know how successfully we are achieving our goals.

Do you consider yourself

☐ of Afro-Caribbean descent

☐ of Indian sub-continent descent

☐ of Asian (Far Eastern) descent

☐ of English, Scottish, Welsh or Irish descent

☐ of other European descent

☐ none of these   I consider myself

[ ]

Are you

☐ a woman ☐ a man

Are you a person with a registered disability?

☐ no, I am not ☐ yes, I am

the nature of your disability

[ ]

the date of your registration

[19]

registration number

[ ]

the date of expiry of your registration

[19]

Royal Mail welcomes applications from disabled people.

Declaration

Please answer truthfully. If any information was found to be false you may be dismissed.

I declare that this information is true and complete

your signature

[ ]

date

[19]

*We need to know if there are any dates when you **couldn't** come to an interview.*

FOR OUR USE ONLY: SOURCE ADV · HDS · TEL · COL · JC · AGCY · OTHER ...

Your record in the community

The form explains here what is meant by a criminal record which is helpful. Being asked about offences is not unusual, especially with jobs that involve working with money or with vulnerable people. Be honest here – some employers will be able to check your record with the police. Indeed some will automatically do so before you are appointed.

Equal opportunities

Some people feel upset about equal opportunities questions. However, as the form says, Royal Mail is working towards equal opportunities. By recording statistics about gender, race and disability they will be able to establish whether their equal opportunities policies are working. This type of question is very often asked by local authorities and an increasing number of other organisations are also taking equal opportunities into account.

Declaration

Simply your signature and the date. Do note the final sentence which asks if there are any dates when you *couldn't* attend an interview. You can provide this information in your covering letter. Don't forget that *all* application forms should be accompanied by a covering letter. Chapter 9 covers this in further detail.

One applicant wrote "I have a good sense of humour – I'm from Liverpool!" It made us smile too, although it didn't necessarily impress us as we are not from Liverpool and wondered if it meant that the writer felt that only Liverpudlians have a sense of humour.

Quote from manager of a small firm

Application form from a small organisation

Having looked at the application form for a large organisation, let's look at one from a company employing eight people. The company specialises in moving freight of various kinds both within the UK and abroad.

Before we look at it, you might like to see the list of questions the managers ask themselves when interviewing candidates. It shows what they are looking for, even at the application stage, and reminds you of the need to always try to get inside the interviewer's head.

Some of these questions may seem unusual – the form is very specifically designed to ensure that they appoint someone who will fit in with the existing work group. The same form is used for all vacancies. This particular company employs young people (no one over 40), mostly men. They are expected to work hard and put in long hours. There is a lot of overlap between each other's work, and people will generally 'muck in' and have a go at anything when necessary. There is a lot of humour in the workplace. There is a high commitment to getting it right, looking after the customer and developing the business.

If you live locally to the company you are applying to, you should be able to find out some of these details if not all. You can find out by:

- word of mouth
- information you can gather when phoning the organisation to get the application form
- asking if your careers office or Jobcentre know of the organisation
- local or national press
- your library.

Obviously no employer is going to give you such a list normally, but you should be able to work out for yourself a fair guess at what their list might be, based on your understanding of the job description and person specification.

Interview checklist

Applicant's name: ....

Question	Yes	No	Comments
Is this person outgoing?			
Is this person shy?			
Is this person ambitious?			
Has this person shown ambition in the past?			
Would this person drive the van and do packing?			
Could this person tolerate _____ (a difficult member of staff)?			
Would our customers like dealing with this person?			
Could this person organise others (international)?			
Does this person seem organised?			
Would this person work long hours?			
Could this person use the computer?			
Will this person understand freight?			
Would this person fit in?			
Do I like this person?			
Will the others like this person?			
Can this person communicate?			
Is this person over-sensitive?			
Has this person got a sense of humour?			

This company actually uses two application forms – applicants have to complete both. The first asks for factual details of name, schools attended, qualifications, etc. Remember when completing this factual information to keep the job description and person specification in mind at all times.

I'm very wary of people who are too obvious when they complete an application form. If they use too many of the words we've used, I think "Oh, he's just read the job description and chucked in a few words."

Quote from a manager at the freight company

As we have already studied these areas using the Royal Mail form, we'll look at the company's other form here.

But before we start you need to know a little about the job itself. There is no person specification although one would be easy to work out from the interview checklist above.

AIRFREIGHT OPERATIONS ASSISTANT
JOB DESCRIPTION

1. Deal with customer orders.
2. Establish how customer requirements can be best met.
3. Identify how to ship goods to their destination.
4. Use computer to record all stages of the customer contract.
5. Drive the van when necessary.
6. Load and unload goods when required.
7. Undertake any other tasks as identified by the management.

APPLICATION FOR EMPLOYMENT.

AIRFREIGHT OPERATIONS ASSISTANT

In order to assist in the selection process we require you to complete both types of application form. The first is a standard format which provides basic information. This second form is designed to find out more in depth information about your past work experience and personality. The greater information that you supply the better the selection process will be. This form completed as honestly and comprehensively as possible will lead to a more satisfactory outcome for you and the company.

1) Which periods of your life were the ones you consider your happiest? Explain why.

2) Please describe situations in your past experience which were the most fulfilling. Explain why.

3) What work situations have been the most difficult to deal with? Explain why they were difficult and what you did to overcome them.

You will see that in the introductory paragraph you are told that the organisation is trying to find out about your past work experience and personality. Their aim is to try to get people to be honest about themselves and their experiences and where possible to get people to drop their application if they feel it is not appropriate. This is an important point that many organisations overlook. If the advertisement is not tailored very tightly to the job and to identifying what the organisation requires of the person, they can find themselves inundated with unsuitable applicants. This is a waste of time for them and also a waste of time for the applicant who has (probably!) put a lot of time and effort into completing the form.

You have been able to sell your skills and talents in the most effective way in the first application form from this company. Now you should work on selling your personality.

1. **Which periods of your life were the ones you consider your happiest? Explain why.**

Gosh, this is difficult to answer. Everyone will have a different happiest time, but here are some ideas to prompt you:

- holidays
- meeting a new girl/boyfriend
- family gatherings
- a particular year at school
- helping in a voluntary capacity.

Don't forget to say why. Was the holiday happy because you had an opportunity to travel with friends around Europe doing your own thing? (If so, this could indicate flexibility.) Be honest in your answer, but keep the details of the job in mind.

2. **Please describe situations in your past experience that were the most fulfilling. Explain why.**

4) What kind of job are you looking for? Explain why.

5) When do you feel most under pressure in or out of work?

6) Britain is in a recession, describe several things that you think will help towards coming out of it.

7) What are your aims and aspirations? What practical steps are you taking to achieve them?

Signed: Dated:

All information submitted by applicants will be treated in strict confidence. This information will not be released to unauthorised persons both in or out of the company.

This appears to be a very similar question to the one above. There is no 'right' way to answer this or any of the other questions. One suggestion here might be to answer the first question with a personal experience and this question with a work experience. You could even mention that this is how you propose to tackle the questions. Some examples of fulfilling work experience would be:

- feeling you've done a job really well
- setting up a new system
- seeing a project through to the end
- helping other people in some way.

3. **What work situations have been the most difficult to deal with? Explain why they were difficult and what you did to overcome them.**

This sort of question can be tricky if you are just beginning your career and feel you have very little to talk about. Nevertheless, you will presumably have had a work placement and perhaps a vacation or part-time job. At the very least you could write about how it felt to settle into the workplace, meeting new people, learning the routines, etc.

'My work placement was in a very busy sales office. The manager was away for my first day, so I felt at a loss.'

'I worked in a home for elderly people and one of the residents, to whom I'd become very attached, had a heart attack when I was in her room.'

'My industrial placement was as a receptionist in a hotel. One of the clients tried to pay by credit card, but the credit card company refused to clear the payment. The customer became very abusive and aggressive as a result.'

'The engineering company I went to was on the verge of going into liquidation when my placement started.'

Why was the experience difficult? Don't write here as if it's all gloom and doom, don't complain about other people, don't run down the organisation. Take some responsibility for your own difficulties without making yourself sound incompetent. Do say very positively how you overcame the difficulties:

'I quickly realised that I could settle into the job better if I understood how the other departments worked. I asked another manager if I could visit the other departments and she agreed to this. I found it very helpful and it gave me a face to put to names on the phone.'

'I called for help and loosened the lady's clothing. I stayed with her until the ambulance arrived.'

'I kept calm and suggested that the angry customer speak to the manager. I showed him into the office and tried to make him feel less uncomfortable.'

'It was very difficult at the engineering company because everyone was so demoralised. However, it seemed to help when I let them know that I felt I could learn a lot from them. I learnt a lot about the way in which businesses operate, too.'

4.   What kind of job are you looking for? Explain why.

Well, obviously you are looking for the job being advertised or you wouldn't be applying. However, this questions really wants a more complete answer. Are you looking for a job that offers:

- excitement?
- challenge?
- routine?
- variety?
- good company?
- good financial rewards?
- valuable experience?

Whichever answer you give (and yours may be different from the above), expand a bit so that the reader gets a real flavour of what you are like as a person.

Rebecca was looking for a job that offered excitement.

5. **When do you feel under most pressure in or out of work?**

Mmm, this is one to be careful with because you could really do damage to your chances of an interview. Keep in mind the organisation. For this company, it wouldn't be wise to say that you felt under pressure when you were too busy, or had to work late or didn't have a fixed routine. In fact there are not many jobs where it would be wise to admit to these problems. You could consider mentioning pressures like:

- being unable to finish the work as well as you'd like
- being unable to use creativity and initiative
- being unchallenged by your work or responsibilities
- having to do repetitive work
- not feeling really involved as part of a team.

6. **Britain is in a recession, describe several things that you think will help towards coming out of it.**

It is reasonable to guess from this question that you would be expected to be aware of current issues, particularly as they relate to British industry. If you don't want to be political about it (and that's always dodgy because the reader's politics may be different from yours) you can do what you've done hundreds of times in essays – discuss both sides of the argument showing that you have a good overview of the situation.

One person simply wrote in answer to this question, "I am a Tory". In fact we were trying, with this question, to establish whether applicants had an awareness of current affairs in the world in general and in business.

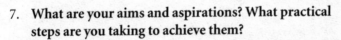

Quote from a manager of the freight company

7. **What are your aims and aspirations? What practical steps are you taking to achieve them?**

Do you know what your aims and aspirations are? Have you a career plan in your head or on paper somewhere? This is a fairly typical interview question if not one often asked on application forms. For that reason, you should spend some time working through where you see yourself in five or ten years, or by the time you retire.

'Safe' aims and aspirations would include:

- ♦♦ working in a job you enjoy
- ♦♦ developing your skills
- ♦♦ climbing a career ladder
- ♦♦ learning about the industry in question.

Have you taken any practical steps? Has the pattern of your education and career to date been logical and focused, or are you still trying to find your niche? Practical steps you may have taken include:

- taking the right courses
- studying hard
- developing relevant skills either through work or in some other way
- finding relevant jobs, even if part-time or vacation work
- learning transferable skills from jobs that were not exactly what you wanted
- learning to use your initiative.

No application form is easy or quick to complete. A more complicated one like this will probably take you several attempts. Look on it in a positive light – if you are offered an interview (and your chances will be greatly increased if you spend the time now), you will have done much of the preparation work for the interview already. (For information on how to handle interviews, see *Excel at Interviews* by Patricia McBride, Hobsons Publishing PLC, 1993.)

Chapter Checklist

When completing your application form, have you:

❏   Taken at least one photocopy before you start? Work on that copy until you are sure you have it exactly right.

❏   Read the instructions on the form carefully and followed them to the letter?

❏   Read the job description, person specification and any information you have about the company thoroughly?

❏   Tried to work out exactly the type of person the organisation is looking for?

❏   Analysed your skills, experience and personality highlighting those which fit in with the needs of the job?

❏   Drafted your answers to the questions on the form?

❏   Been consistent with the way you present material? Make it easy for the reader to work through it.

❏   Left the form after the first draft so that you have an opportunity to re-think what you've written?

❏   Polished the form until you are completely happy that it gets across exactly the message you want?

❏   Made a good copy with no mistakes?

❏   Remembered your covering letter?

9 The Covering Letter

You should read this chapter:

- ↠ when you have completed your CV or application form.

By the end of this chapter you should know:

- ↠ what points to consider when writing a covering letter
- ↠ who to address the letter to
- ↠ how to write letters when applying for a specific job
- ↠ how to write letters speculatively.

The importance of covering letters

Covering letters are strange things – it's often difficult to know what to include, but it's definitely not done not to send one. Your covering letter is as important as your CV. Together they can make a winning team.

The covering letter is an opportunity to further sell *yourself* as a person, as well as to highlight any major points you think will impress.

Making a start

By the time you get to read this chapter you have probably spent some time preparing your CV or completing your application form and you're probably thinking 'I can't think of another word to say!' Sorry – but you have to . . .

If you are sending a CV, you may have chosen to leave out some of the 'Additional Information' at the end of your CV to form the meat of your covering letter. If you've completed an application form, the odds are that the layout of the form didn't give you much opportunity to say everything you want to say.

But let's do the easy bit first. Whether you are writing in response to a particular job advert or speculatively you must get the letter to the correct person. This may be obvious if the name was stated in the advertisement or was sent to you with information from the organisation. However, if it wasn't or if you are writing speculatively, spend the time and effort to find out who the correct person is. It's a small point, but it does show the reader that you are able to use your initiative. You simply have to phone the organisation and ask the switchboard who would be the correct person.

Daniel knew how important it was to get his application to the right person.

Be prepared though. Often switchboard operators don't listen well and before you know where you are they've put you through to the personnel manager (or whoever) without having given you their name or having been requested to do so. So instead of a nice informal chat to the operator, you're speaking instantly to the decision maker. If that leaves you saying 'Um, um' a few times, you won't make a good impression. It would make sense, therefore, to prepare what you would say if this happens.

If you are inexperienced at speaking to people in 'author-ity', make a few notes of what you want to say:

➤➤ what job you are interested in – also noting where you found out about the job and any job reference number there may be

➤➤ some basic facts about yourself that relate to the job

➤➤ why you are interested in the job.

Have these notes ready *before* you dial!

I admire people for going for jobs a little above their present experience level. However, people must have the absolute basics. I advertised for a job recently where it was stated that the post-holder would need excellent oral and written skills. Someone wrote in their covering letter, "I am not very good at expressing myself on paper due to a poor education".

Quote from a manager

Practical issues

Your covering letter should be on good quality A4 paper, preferably the same as your CV if you've sent one. *Don't* use small coloured writing pads, lined A4 paper with holes punched down the side, pretty floral paper Aunt Mary sent you last Christmas or anything else. It won't impress and you'll simply look unprofessional.

Layout for letters is usually *blocked*, that means:

1. no indents.
2. everything lined up to the left and right.

Also:

1. Punctuation marks are not used after the address.
2. The date is written in full but without 'st', 'nd', etc.
3. The main heading is highlighted in some way, usually with bold type. If you are handwriting the letter (and some employers ask you to do this), the heading can be written in capitals or underlined.
4. It is a convention to use 'Yours sincerely' if you write to a person by name. If you really can't find out the person's name, you should address your letter 'Dear Sir or Madam', and end 'Yours faithfully'.
5. Write Enc. at the bottom of your letter to show that you have enclosed something (your CV, application form or anything else).
6. Remember to include your telephone number in the letter somewhere, either under your address or in the body of the letter. Make it easy for them to phone you.

Here is an example:

```
Bloggs Engineering Works
Unit 7
St Martins Industrial Estate
Bloxburg
Avon BB22 3EE

Your address
etc
postcode

22 July 1994

Dear Ms Stedman

Vacancy for Trainee Engineer

Opening comments.

Body of your letter, may take one or more paragraphs.

Final sentence, including telephone numbers.

Yours sincerely

Your name

Enc
```

Occasionally you will be asked to write the covering letter by hand. Generally this means that they want to check your handwriting either because:

1. they want to ensure that it is legible, or
2. they plan to get a graphologist to check it to make an assessment of your personality!

Graphology isn't used terribly widely so it's more likely to be the first reason. Obviously this means that you need to use your 'best' handwriting.

Whether your letter is hand-written, typed or word processed make sure that it is grammatically correct. If you are unsure, ask someone you trust to check your letter.

Content

Your covering letter should sound confident and lively. It should tell the reader in very brief terms (using bullet points or not), why you'd be good for the job.

So polish your selling skills again. Don't overdo it and look pushy or big-headed, but simply let them know what you can do. This means that you have to summarise in four or five sentences what you've said in the CV or application form. You may choose to add some new information, perhaps the fact that you'd like to move to that area or when you are available for interview. Remember to use all those positive sounding words again.

On the next few pages are some advertisements and the covering letter to go with each one.

Assistant Secretary

Hawkins Ltd requires an assistant secretary to provide secretarial and administrative support. The duties are varied and will include typing, arranging meetings and taking minutes.

Applicants should have a good standard of education, with GCSE/GCE English and RSA Typewriting or similar, excellent communication skills and be able to word process.

Applications in writing, including full CV and details of two referees, should be sent to:

Ms M Ahmed, Personnel Manager, Hawkins Ltd,
Peterson Road, Oxford

Dear Mrs Ahmed

Vacancy for Assistant Secretary

Please find enclosed my CV in application for the above vacancy which was advertised in this week's *Oxford Reporter*.[1] As you will see, I am just about to leave the Regional College having completed a BTEC Secretarial course.[2] The course included a work placement where I was given valuable experience in all the areas outlined in your advertisement.[3]

I am particularly interested in working for Hawkins as I know several people who work for the company and believe it to be an excellent company to work for.[4]

I am a hard working person, able to work unsupervised once I 'know the ropes' although I also enjoy working as part of a team.[5] My communication skills are good – I have been Chairperson of the Students Association for the past 18 months.[6]

I look forward to hearing from you.[7] I am available for interview after the 22nd or earlier by arrangement.[8]

Yours sincerely

This is a pretty good letter, bouncy and confident:

1. The applicant has remembered to mention where he or she saw the job advertised.
2. This should be more specific – which BTEC secretarial course?
3. The applicant could have enlarged on this a little, perhaps repeating the tasks as outlined in the advertisement for emphasis.
4. There's no harm in a bit of flattery, but don't overdo it.
5. This sentence highlights personal strengths all employers would value.
6. Although this information would probably be in the CV it's worth repeating here to emphasise the point.
7. Sounds confident without being pushy.
8. This sounds as if you have other things going on in your life. To simply say 'I'm available any time' sounds as if you have no calls on your time at all (this may be true but you don't say so).

Direct Marketing Assistant

Griffin Ltd are looking for a well motivated and enthusiastic person to join their small marketing department.

The person appointed will be part of a team responsible for the direct marketing promotion of the company.

We are looking for someone with an interest in learning how to:

Copywrite and proof-read
Analyse campaign data
Liaise with other departments and printers

You should be a good communicator both verbally and in writing. Keyboard skills are an advantage.

Please send your CV and covering letter to:
John Farnsworth, Griffin Ltd, 27 Dallow Road, York

Dear Mr Farnsworth

Direct Marketing Assistant

Please find enclosed my CV in application of the above job advertised in this week's *Recorder*.

I have recently left Colmsford Regional College where I successfully completed a BTEC in Business Studies.[1] I particularly enjoyed the module on marketing.[2] and went on to do a six-week placement with Briggs' Hardware in their Marketing Department.[3]

[4]While at Briggs, I learnt how to use word processing and desk top publishing programs.[5] Last year I was deputy editor of the student magazine and these skills were fully tested there![6]

I would love[7] to work in direct marketing, especially at Griffins, as I feel it is an exciting field at the moment.[8]

Yours sincerely

Well, as an employer I'd be reaching for the phone to see this person . . .

1. Two selling points in one sentence. He or she has 'successfully' completed the course (positive word) and mentioned a very relevant course, too.

2. Likewise, 'enjoyed' and mentioned the most relevant module.

3. This placement must have offered a lot of valuable skills, pity they weren't mentioned in a little more detail.

4. He or she has managed to avoid starting two consecutive paragraphs with 'I'.

5. This is a higher level of computer literacy than many college leavers and is certainly worth highlighting.

6. A little humour doesn't hurt, and this is connected directly to really useful experience editing a magazine

7. Is this a bit gushing? Perhaps, but it comes across as sincere and enthusiastic.

8. Why is it an exciting field 'at the moment'. To finish the sentence by briefly saying why would demonstrate up to date knowledge and be a bonus.

Trainee Windscreen Fitter

Screensafe plc are looking for a trainee to join their team of windscreen fitters. Body shop experience would be an advantage.

Please apply to:

Screensafe plc
Screensafe House
66-71 High Street
Northton

Dear Mr Proto[1]

[2]

I am writing to apply for your job as a Trainee Windscreen Fitter.[3] I think I would enjoy this sort of work as I spend a lot of time helping family and friends to repair their cars.[4] I also go to Car Maintenance classes at Coltree Evening Centre.[5]

I am enclosing my CV and hope to hear from you soon.[6]

Yours sincerely,

This letter certainly gives a lot of useful information but could be improved nevertheless:

1. The writer has bothered to phone Screensafe and find out who to address the letter to. This shows initiative.
2. Always put a heading on your covering letter. It makes it easier to read and refer to. If the organisation is advertising several vacancies it makes it easier for them to keep track of which letters belong where.
3. The writer should tell the employer where he or she saw the advertisement. This helps employers to decide their most effective way of telling the world about their vacancy which may help them in the future.
4. This sentence is both good and bad. It comes across as enthusiastic and that's always good, but it also seems rather as if the applicant is telling the employer what they can do for him or her rather than what he or she can do for them. Perhaps it could be re-worded along the lines of, '*I have experience of stripping engines and replacing spare parts. I have helped re-spray an old Mini. I very much enjoy this type of work and go to Car . . .*'
5. Good to mention evening class, it shows real commitment.
6. Why not make this last sentence more sparky? '*I am enclosing my CV and hope you will feel that I have the qualities to make a good windscreen fitter.*'

HIGH MEADOWS HOUSING

CUSTOMER SERVICES CLERK

We are looking for someone aged between 17 and 25 to fill this very important post. The job involves taking customer details, quoting prices and inputting data on to computer. The ability to deal tactfully with other companies and departments as well as with customers is vital.

Previous experience of this type of work would be an advantage.

Contact:

Mrs Mari Singh, Customer Services Manager
High Meadows Housing, High Meadows, Clydesfield

Dear Mrs Singh

re: Customer Services Clerk

Your advertisement in this week's *Recorder* interests me very much. I am currently working as an Administrative Assistant for Briggs Ltd and feel that I have very relevant skills[1] for this vacancy:

- ↔ I am experienced at dealing with customers
- ↔ I am familiar with word processing and accounts packages on IBM compatible machines
- ↔ I am used to liaising with other departments.[2]

I am enclosing my CV and hope that you will give me an interview.[3]

Yours sincerely

This is one way to lay out a covering letter – using bullet points to highlight your skills. Here are some points you may have noticed about this letter:

1. This is a confident sentence that should keep the reader reading.
2. Good list of skills. The writer hasn't pointed out that he or she has no experience of giving quotes, it's simply implied by omission. That's fine because the advertisement only says 'previous experience would be an advantage' so they'll be willing to give someone training if necessary.
3. Although the list of skills is good, there is no mention of personal qualities. From the advertisement I am sure the post-holder would need tact, good attention to detail, ability to keep calm under stress, good communication skills. The writer could have mentioned these even if they are already in the CV. Remember, if the employer gets a huge response they may not bother to read the CV if the covering letter is poor.

People write some strange things on covering letters sometimes. One person wrote, "I would really like this job (and that's the first time I've written that)".

Quote from a personnel manager

SCHUMACHER LTD

are looking for

MACHINE/SETTER OPERATORS
to work as part of a team in our
busy production department

You will need the ability to use simple tools to ensure that all
our machinery is kept in good running order. Full training
will be given although you must be capable of working on
your own initiative once trained. The job involves heavy
lifting. You must be literate and numerate and able to pass an
aptitude text.

Hours 6 am–3 pm or 3 pm–10 pm

Contact
The Personnel Department
Schumacher Ltd
Smyth Industrial Estate
Colmsworth
Wilts

Dear Mr McGregor[1]

[2]

I am writting[3] about your job in the *Recorder* for a
Machine Setter/Operator.[4]

Please find enclosed my CV. I am leaving school next
month and think I would be good at this sort of work.[5]

I hope you will consider me for an interview.[6]

Yours faithfully[7]

Oops! I doubt if this person would get an interview if
there was much other choice.

1. This shows initiative, because the advertisement
   didn't show the name of the person to contact and
   the applicant has bothered to find out.
2. No heading!
3. Not good enough. The advertisement states that
   they're looking for someone who is literate. This
   person should have asked someone to check his or
   her spelling before sending the letter off.

4. This sentence is poorly worded. It was an *advertisement* for a Setter/Operator, not a job for one.
5. Mmm, so the person thinks they'd be good for the job, but has completely failed to convince the reader of the fact. He or she should have said why they thought they were suitable.
6. This sounds a bit grovelling. The sentence could be re-worded to sound more positive. Perhaps something like 'I am sure you will agree that I have potential for this type of work and hope you will grant me an interview.'
7. Because the letter starts *Dear Mr McGregor*, it should end with *Yours sincerely*, not *Yours faithfully*.

DISPATCHER

Are you enthusiastic, neat and articulate? Do you have a good telephone manner? We are looking for someone to help in the daily picking and packing of our products for shipment all over the country. Full training will be given but previous dispatch experience would be helpful. Starting salary according to experience and age.

This position would suit a school leaver.

Write in the first instance to:
Mr Robert Chalmers
Dispatch Manager
Dyers of Lolswitch
Cowley Road
Lolswitch
LS4 4PP

Dear Mr Chalmers

Dispatcher vacancy

I am very interested in the above vacancy which was advertised in this week's Lolswitch News.[1]

I am an enthusiastic[2] and energetic school leaver, punctual and reliable.[3] Although I have not done dispatch work before[4] I have worked in a shoe shop on Saturdays.[5]

I am enclosing my CV which I hope[6] you will find interesting and hope[7] to hear from you soon.

Yours sincerely

Not a bad letter, but it could be improved a lot. Let's look at it point by point:

1. Often companies will want to know where you have learnt about a vacancy as it helps with their marketing.

2. It's useful to try to 'feed back' to the employer some of the words they've used in the advertisement. It helps them to feel at ease with your application.

3. This is good – four positive, personal qualities sold in one sentence.

4. Golden rule – don't highlight what you *haven't* done. Let them find that out by reading your CV (or they may not bother to read it . . .). Emphasise instead what you *have* done.

5. It's fine to mention previous work experience but *make the links.* This sentence could read '*I have experience of working with others and controlling stock through my work as a Saturday Sales Assistant during my last two years at school.*'

6. This sentence sounds a bit feeble and could be much more punchy.

7. 'Hope' used twice in the same sentence. A final punchy sentence could be: '*I am very interested in working for your company which has a good reputation. I believe my CV will show that I have many of the qualities you seek and I look forward to hearing from you.*'

 I advertised for a fairly high level post and was amazed at the poor presentation of some of the CVs and covering letters I received. One person had actually written on their covering letter "I don't know what I can

bring to the organisation".
Frankly, if he didn't know,
why should I bother to try to
find out!

Quote from an employer

Covering letters sent 'on spec'

So far in the chapter, we have assumed that you will be applying for an advertised job. However, this is not always the case. If you don't see any suitable jobs to apply for it is well worth considering writing to organisations asking if they have any work. For example, if you want to get into hotel management, you could write to all the big hotel chains and indeed your local hotels asking what openings they have. You have nothing to lose and perhaps a lot to gain.

The worst that can happen is that your information will be put in the bin or sent back. The best is that you are offered an interview immediately. More likely, the company will write back saying that they're holding your details on file. Hopefully, they will then contact you when a vacancy occurs.

If you are writing 'on spec' be clear about what sort of job you are asking for, or say if you are willing to consider anything they might have to offer. If you are looking for a particular type of work write the letter very much with that in mind in the way suggested already in this chapter.

So to write a speculative letter, you should start something like:

Dear Mr Smith

Secretarial vacancies

I am writing to ask if you have any secretarial vacancies at the moment. I have . . .

From there the letter can continue in much the same way as any other covering letter.

If you are willing to consider any work the company has to offer you can add as a final line (or elsewhere if it fits better):

If you have no secretarial vacancies at present I would also like to be considered for any clerical/typist posts available.

Be polite, but don't be horribly humble, or you will seem terribly lacking in confidence in your ability to get a job.

Targeted 'on spec' letters

An alternative way to write 'on spec' letters is to target them to a particular organisation as a response to something you know about the company. This could be an article you have seen in a newspaper or trade or professional magazine, or something you have learnt about by word of mouth. Here are a few beginnings of such letters to demonstrate the point:

Dear Mr Thomas

*I read with interest in this week's **Daily Telegraph** that your company has just won a big contract to supply Hokomoto with parts for their engines. It occurs to me that in the light of your increased workload you may be looking for more administrative staff. I am . . .*

or

Dear Ms Cohen

*This week's **Hotels Monthly** mentions that you are planning to open a hotel in my area within the next three months. I have recently finished . . .*

or

Dear Miss Schultz

Now that the housing market is finally picking up I am

writing to ask whether you anticipate taking on any additional staff. I am . . .

or

Dear Mr Briggs
This week's **Bloxford Recorder** *mentioned that your company is planning to expand into other areas of the fashion industry. I am a . . .*

By responding to changes in the circumstances of an organisation, you will be showing that you have your ear to the ground, and have read the right newspapers and journals. It also shows considerable initiative. Both of these would impress most employers. Almost certainly the worst that could happen is that your letter would go on file.

Blowing all the rules

If, *if*, you are really desperate, have tried everything else and failed, or you seek work in a creative field and are exceptionally original, consider breaking all the rules so far outlined in this chapter. Can you write a covering letter that will make you stand out by its sheer originality and creativity? Try to link it to the type of work you want to do:

- Want to work in publishing?
  Design yourself a book cover with your details on the back!
- Want to work in advertising?
  Write an advertisement for yourself.
- Want to work in graphic design?
  Design a poster telling about yourself.
- Want to work in fabric design?
  Send a sample of fabric you've made, perhaps incorporating your name.

Don't automatically assume this will work, or feel devastated if you get a poor response – but if you've tried

Sarah knew the benefits of targeting her application.

everything else all you've got to lose is your pride . . .

Here's a real-life story about two young men who decided to take an alternative approach.

Jon and Michael had just finished college and wanted to get into the advertising business in the middle of the longest recession Britain has known since the 1930s. The advertising industry is in a bad way. Staff are being laid off rather than being taken on. Very, very few jobs are advertised and they didn't even manage to get an interview for those few jobs they could find to apply for.

Things were desperate. But they were determined. This is what they did.

They found out the names of 23 advertising agencies in their area that they would like to work for and identified the name of the key person to approach in each agency (all were men). Jon and Michael then bought some pink scented writing paper and envelopes and a green pen. As well as the usual address on the front of each envelope they wrote *PERSONAL* in big letters. They tried to make the handwriting look feminine. This ensured that Mr Big's secretary wouldn't open the letter and that it would be opened directly by Mr Big himself.

Inside they placed a photo of themselves taken in a photo booth. They were informal photos in which they tried to look like brothers on a day out. The letter (again written in green ink) which went with the photo was along the lines of:

Dear Mr _____
I don't know if you remember that evening in a Brighton car park 22 years ago, but our mother Janie certainly remembers you.

(They'd got his attention by now!) From there they managed to turn the letter into a funny plea for an interview for a job. Of the 23 agencies they approached, 22 offered them interviews and four offered jobs . . .

Why was this approach so successful? Remember – they were looking for jobs in a creative industry. Their approach was very creative. Any potential employer would be sensible enough to think 'If they can be this creative to get to see me they'll also be creative working for me'.

Remember too, they had little to lose. They'd tried everything else and were willing to take the risk.

Here's another story along similar lines. This time it involves a man who wanted to get his script read by a film director. He knew that the director would not look at any scripts unless they came through an agent and this man couldn't get on an agent's books: stalemate.

He discovered (somehow) that it took the director 43 seconds to drive from the security gate of the studio to his parking spot. He also found out that the director usually arrived at work between five and six in the morning (!). The guards at the security gate were under strict instructions not to accept any post that looked as if it could contain a script, so that option was out. Instead, the author arrived at the studio at 4.30 in the morning and gave the guard a small package (clearly no script inside) saying that the director was expecting to collect this letter at the gate when he arrived.

When the director arrived, the guard passed it on. The director looked at it. Underneath his name was written in small letters *'If you have 43 seconds to spare, open this envelope'*. Inside was an audio tape. Who could resist listening to this mysterious tape? The director listened. It was 43 seconds of soundtrack from a movie of the script the man had written. Of course, the movie didn't exist yet, just 43 seconds of the soundtrack. He'd gone to the expense of getting the soundtrack made and done a good job of it.

The director was impressed and agreed to read the script. The gamble paid off.

Chapter Checklist

Do you understand that you should:

❑ Always write a covering letter – they are the other half of your application, whether by CV or form? The exception is for college applications.

❑ Use good quality A4 paper?

❑ Not to use more than one side of A4 paper?

❑ Make sure your handwriting can be read?

❑ Find out who to address the letter to?

❑ Remember to head the letter with the job title?

❑ Sign letters addressed to a named person, 'Yours sincerely'.

❑ Use the letter to provide information about yourself otherwise missing or to highlight particular important points?

❑ Consider using bullet points if you want to get a lot of information across?

❑ Sound positive and confident, not grovelling and apologetic?

❑ Make sure the letter is articulate, pleasant to read, clean and perfect?

❑ Not forget that writing to organisations 'on spec' can often pay off?

150144